Hola!

First, let me introduce myself. I am Ana Regalado; many of you may know me as Salty Cocina from my social media platforms. If you are reading this, congratulations! You have purchased my very first cookbook! You have no idea how exciting this is for my family and me. Let me tell you why. First, grab a cafecito, because this may take a while.

I was born in Zacatecas, Mexico, in a tiny town called Cruces. At that time, the home we lived in did not have running water or electricity. I remember my mom, dad, and older brothers carrying water from the well to the house for washing dishes and cooking. Even though I lived there for a short seven years, it left a significant imprint in my heart. We didn't have the luxuries we have in the US, but I have the best memories and many involved foods. I love everything about my Mexican culture, especially the food! I have always had an interest in the kitchen, ever since I was a little girl. I loved being in the kitchen with my mom or Abuelita as they prepared simple but very delicious meals on their wooden stoves. Each time I smell a dish they would make, that delightful smell transports me back to that moment in time.

I began making Tiktok videos after my children introduced me to the Application. During this time, Covid emerged, and everyone went under quarantine. Life was full of uncertainty, so I began posting my recipes on Tiktok, then Youtube, and on Instagram. With so many people dying from this virus, I was unsure what the future would hold for me. Imagine how amazing it would be to have your mom, grandma, or great-grandma, always guiding you in the kitchen? Hearing her voice as she explains her recipes, that's what I want to leave my kids and everyone else who wishes to use and enjoy them and make beautiful memories with their families!

Ana Regalado.
Salty Cocina

TABLE OF CONTENTS

TABLE OF CONTENTS

STRAWBERRY HORCHATA

By Salty Cocina

INGREDIENTS

- 6 CUPS WATER (DIVIDED)
- 2 CUPS WHOLE MILK
- 12 OZ CAN EVAPORATED MILK
- 14 OZ CAN CONDENSED MILK OR SWEETENER OF YOUR CHOICE
- 1 LB OF FRESH RIPE STRAWBERRIES (MORE FOR GARNISHING)
- 1 CUP LONG GRAIN WHITE RICE
- 1-2 STICK OF CINNAMON
- 1 TBSP VANILLA (OPTIONAL)
- BLENDER

MAKES 8-10 SERVINGS

INSTRUCTIONS

1. Rinse the rice until the water runs clear and soak in 1-1/2-2 cups of hot water with the cinnamon for 2-3 hours.
2. Disinfect the strawberries in water and one tsp of salt for 10 minutes, rinse them and hull them.
3. Pour the rice, water, and cinnamon sticks into the blender and blend for a minute or until smooth.
4. Strain the contents into the pitcher and add six additional cups of water.
5. Blend the strawberries (save some for garnishing)
6. Mix the blended strawberries with the rice water and add the evaporated milk, whole milk, condensed milk, and vanilla.
7. Serve over ice with and garnish with diced strawberries
8. ENJOY!

NOTE: leave out the strawberries to make regular horchata.

CHOCOLATE HORCHATA

By Salty Cocina

INGREDIENTS

- 1 1/2 CUPS LONG GRAIN WHITE RICE
- 2 STICKS OF CINNAMON
- 1 DISC MEXICAN CHOCOLATE OR COCOA
- 6-7 CUPS OF WATER (DIVIDED)
- 12 OZ CAN EVAPORATED MILK
- 7 OZ CONDENSED MILK OR HALF CUP OF SUGAR
- 1 TSP VANILLA

MAKES 6-8 SERVINGS

INSTRUCTIONS

1. Rinse the rice until the water runs clear
2. Soak the rice and the cinnamon sticks in 1-1/2-2 cups of hot water for 2-3 hours
3. Transfer the rice along with the water cinnamon sticks and the chocolate disc to the blender. Blend for 1 minute or until smooth
4. Strain the contents into the pitcher add six cups of water, evaporated milk, condensed milk or sugar, and vanilla. Mix the ingredients, taste, and adjust the sweetness if needed.
5. Serve over ice and sprinkle with chocolate or cinnamon.
6. ENJOY!

CUCUMBER & LIME AGUA FRESCA

By Salty Cocina

INGREDIENTS

- 8 CUPS WATER (DIVIDED)
- 3 CUCUMBERS
- 1/2 CUP LIME JUICE
- SWEETENER OF YOUR CHOICE

MAKES 6-8 SERVINGS

INSTRUCTIONS

1. Wash and peel 2 1/2 of the cucumbers; reserve half for garnishing the drink. Using a spoon, scrape out the seeds, roughly chop them, and add them to the blender.
2. Slice the remaining half of the cucumber into thin slices (do not peel)
3. Blend the cucumbers with 2 cups of water, then transfer the ingredients into a pitcher.
4. Add in the remainder of the water, lime juice, and the cucumber slices.
5. Sweeten with a sweetener of your choice.
6. Serve over lots of ice and Enjoy!

OPTIONAL- Blend ONE of the lime rinds with a cup of water and strain it into the pitcher! This will not make it taste bitter but it will add much more flavor to your agua fresca!

CHERRY LIMEADE

By Salty Cocina

INGREDIENTS

- 2 CUPS FRESH OR
  FROZEN CHERRIES
- 1 CUP FRESH
  SQUEEZED LIME
  JUICE (6-8 LIMES)
  EXTRA FOR
  GARNISHING THE
  PEEL FROM ONE
  LIME SWEETENER
  OF CHOICE
- 8 -10 CUPS OF
  WATER (DIVIDED)

MAKES 8-10 SERVINGS
PREP TIME: 25 MINUTES

INSTRUCTIONS

1. If using fresh cherries, disinfect them by soaking them in water with one tbsp
of vinegar or salt for 10 minutes
2. Rinse them and remove the seeds
3. Squeeze out the juice from 6-8 limes or until you have 1 cup of lime juice
4. Blend the cherries, the rind from one lime, a sweetener of your choice, and
 two cups of water
5. Strain the contents from the blender into a pitcher
6. Mix in the lime juice and six additional cups of water
7. Serve over ice and garnish with thinly sliced limes and maraschino cherries.

TAMARIND AGUA FRESCA

By Salty Cocina

INGREDIENTS

- 10-12 TAMARINDO PODS
- 7 OZ PILONCILLO, OR A SWEETENER OF YOUR CHOICE
- 14 QUARTS OF WATER (DIVIDED)

You can find Tamarindo pods in most Mexican markets. recommend making this drink out of fresh pods rather than the ready-to-make tamarind paste for the best possible flavor.

PREP TIME: TIME: 10 MINUTES
COOK TIME: 1 HR 15 MINUTES
TOTAL TIME: 1 HR 25 MINUTES
10-12 SERVINGS

INSTRUCTIONS

1. Remove the hard shells and fibers from the pods and give them a good rinse.
2. Boil over medium/high heat for 12-15 minutes, cover, and soak for one hour.
3. Squeeze out the seeds from the pods and remove any visible fibers.
4. Blend the pods along with the water from the stockpot.
5. Strain the tamarind into a pitcher
6. If using piloncillo, boil in two cups of water until it's completely dissolved and add it to the pitcher.
7. Add ice, the remainder of the water, and a sweetener of your choice.
8. Enjoy!

ICED CAFE DE OLLA

By Salty Cocina

INGREDIENTS

- 8 CUPS WATER
- 2 STICKS OF CINNAMON
- 4 WHOLE CLOVES
- 7 OZ OF PILONCILLO OR ONE CUP BROWN SUGAR
- 12 OZ CAN EVAPORATED MILK
- 1 TSP VANILLA
- 2 CUPS WHOLE MILK
- 1/2 CUP CONDENSED MILK (OPTIONAL)
- 1/2 CUP INSTANT COFFEE

Other suggested ingredients:

Ice, Caramel, Ground Cinnamon, and Whip Cream

PREP TIME: 10
COOK TIME: 20MINS
TOTAL TIME: 30MINS
MAKES 10-12 SERVINGS

INSTRUCTIONS

1. Boil the water with the cinnamon, cloves, and the piloncillo for 10-12 minutes in a medium saucepan.
2. Add the 1/2 cup of your favorite instant coffee (8-10 tbsp)
3. Cool down for 1 -2 hrs.
4. Mix in the evaporated milk, condensed milk, vanilla, and the whole milk to the cold coffee,
5. Drizzle your glass with caramel, serve over ice and top off with whip cream or cinnamon.
6. ENJOY!

CINNAMON BANANA AGUA FRESCA

By Salty Cocina

INGREDIENTS

- 2 RIPE BANANAS
- 12 OZ CAN EVAPORATED MILK
- 1 CUP WHOLE MILK
- 1 TSP VANILLA
- 1 TSP CINNAMON
- SWEETENER OF YOUR CHOICE OF CONDENSED MILK
- 5 CUPS WATER

MAKES 6-8 SERVINGS
PREP TIME: 15 MINUTES

INSTRUCTIONS

1. Blend the bananas with evaporated milk, whole milk, cinnamon, vanilla, and sweetener.
2. Pour the ingredient from the blender into a pitcher and add 5 cups of water.
3. Pour over ice and sprinkle with ground cinnamon.
4. Enjoy

CREAMY STRAWBERRY AGUA FRESCA

By Salty Cocina

INGREDIENTS

- 2 LBS STRAWBERRIES
- 1 1/2 LITERS OF WATER (DIVIDED)
- 14 OZ CAN CONDENSED MILK
- 12 OZ. AN EVAPORATED MILK
- 4 CUPS WHOLE MILK
- 1 TSP VANILLA
- ONE .58 OZ ENVELOPE OF STRAWBERRY FLAVORED DRINK MIX OR FOOD COLORING (OPTIONAL)
- ICE

MAKES
16 (8OZ) SERVINGS

INSTRUCTIONS

1. Disinfect the strawberries in water and one tsp salt or three tbsp of vinegar
2. Trim and Hull cut the strawberries in half for more effortless blending and reserve a few to garnish the glass and pitcher.
3. Blend the strawberries with two cups of water
4. Pour the ingredients from the blender into a pitcher and mix in the rest of the ingredients.
5. Taste and adjust the level of sweetness if needed by adding more water or a sweetener of your choice.
6. Enjoy over ice with diced strawberries.

PUMPKIN SPICED HORCHATA

By Salty Cocina

HORCHATA INGREDIENTS

- 1 CUP LONG-GRAIN OR REGULAR WHITE RICE
- 1 STICK OF CINNAMON
- 1-1/2 CUPS HOT WATER
- 12 OZ CAN EVAPORATED MILK
- 14 OZ CAN CONDENSED MILK
- 6 CUPS OF WATER
- 1 TSP VANILLA
- 1 TSP PUMPKIN SPICE
- 2 CUPS OF WHOLE MILK
- 1 CUP PUMPKIN PUREE
- GROUND CINNAMON FOR GARNISHING

MAKES 10-12 8OZ SERVINGS

INSTRUCTIONS

1. Soak the rice and cinnamon stick in 1-1/2 cups of hot water. You can also soak the rice in room temperature water and refrigerator overnight.
2. Blend the rice, water, cinnamon stick, pumpkin spice for 1-2 minutes or until smooth.
3. Using a fine-mesh strainer, strain the rice mixture into a pitcher. Using a spatula, move the mixture around and slowly pour an additional six cups of water through the stainer. Continue to stir the mixture until all you have left is the residue. If making atole, reserve the rice residue.
4. Add the evaporated milk, condensed milk, vanilla, and two cups of milk.
5. Mix until all the ingredients are well Incorporated.
6. Pour over ice and garnish with ground cinnamon.

PUMPKIN SPICED ATOLE

By Salty Cocina

ATOLE INGREDIENTS

- RICE RESIDUE FROM THE HORCHATA
- 2 CUPS OF WATER
- 1/2 CUP PUMPKIN PUREE
- 1 TSP VANILLA
- 4-5 CUPS OF WHOLE MILK
- 1/2 CUP OF SUGAR OR A SWEETENER OF YOUR CHOICE

MAKES6-8 SERVINGS

INSTRUCTIONS

1. In a medium saucepan, heat 2 cups of water over medium heat. Mix in the rice residue from the horchata. If using corn starch, mix it in before heating the water.
2. Mix in 1/2 cup pumpkin puree, 1 tsp vanilla, 1/2 cup of sugar, and 4-5 cups of whole milk.
3. Bring to a simmer and boil on low heat for 8-10 minutes with constant movement. Adjust the thickness by adding more milk if needed.
4. Serve warm and sprinkle with ground cinnamon.
5. Enjoy with your favorite pan dulce!

Note: You can also substitute the rice residue with 2-3 tbsp of corn starch.

Antojitos
Mexicanos

HOMEMADE-CHICHARRONES

By Salty Cocina

INGREDIENTS

PREPARATION:30 MIN
COOKING: 1HR 15 MIN
READY IN: 1 HR 45 MIN

- 7-10 LBS PIG FAT, PORK SKIN OR PORK BELLY
- 1/3 CUP APPLE CIDER OR REGULAR VINEGAR
- 1/2 CUP WATER
- 1/2 TBSP SALT

Note: The water helps the pork from sticking to the bottom of the pan before it releases the fat. After 20 minutes, the water will completely simmer down and the chicharrones will cook in the fat released from the pig fat.

INSTRUCTIONS

1. Soak pork fat in vinegar and water for 20-30 minutes. Rinse and cut it into 1-2 inch pieces.
2. Add the pork into a dutch oven pan or a heavy bottom pan.
3. Dissolve the salt in 1/2 cup of water and pour it over the pig fat.
4. Cook over medium/high heat for a total of 1 hr 15 minutes with frequent movement. After 20-30 minutes, turn the heat to low and continue cooking until they reach a golden color.
5. As you remove them from the pot, set them in a dish lined with a clean paper towel to soak off the excess grease.
6. Once the fat rendered from the chicharrones cools down, transfer it to a container and use it to prepare other dishes. (refried beans, tamales, etc.)

BEEF ENCHILADAS

By Salty Cocina

INGREDIENTS

- 1 LB LEAN GROUND BEEF
- 2 JALAPEÑOS OR BELL PEPPER
- 1/4 ONION E
- 2 GARLIC CLOVES
- 1 TSP CUMIN
- 1/2 TSP OREGANO
- SALT & PEPPER
- 1 TBSP CHILI POWDER
- 8OZ CAN TOMATO SAUCE
- 12-14 CORN OR FLOUR TORTILLAS
- VEGETABLE OIL FOR FRYING
- YOUR FAVORITE MELTING CHEESE
- (MONTEREY JACK, PEPPER JACK, OAXACA, MOZARELLA, ETC.)

*TOPPING SUGGESTIONS
RED ONION, CILANTRO,
LETTUCE, QUESO FRESCO,
QUESO COTIJA,
AVOCADO, RADISHES*

ENCHILADA SAUCE INGREDIENTS

- 6-8 CHILE GUAJILLO, NM CHILI PODS, OR CALIFORNIA CHILI PODS
- 5-6 CHILES DE ARBOL FOR SPICE
- (OPTIONAL)
- 1-2 GARLIC CLOVES
- 1/4 TSP CUMIN
- 1/2 TSP OREGANO
- 1 TBSP CHICKEN BOUILLON
- 2 CUPS CHICKEN BROTH

**PREPARATION: 30 MIN
COOKING: 20 MIN
READY IN: 50 MIN**

INTRUCTIONS

1. Remove the stems and seeds from the chile guajillos and soak them in hot water along with the chiles de Arbol for 15 minutes or until pliable.
2. Blend the peppers along with two garlic cloves, oregano, and two cups of chicken broth.
3. Strain it into a saucepan, season with ground cumin and chicken bouillon, and simmer for 8-10 minutes over low/med heat.
4. In a medium, pan brown the ground beef and add the minced onion, jalapeños, garlic, tomato sauce, and seasonings. Simmer over medium heat for 8-10 minutes or until the sauce simmers down.
5. Lightly fry the tortilla until pliable, dip it into the enchilada sauce, add the meat and spoonful of cheese. Roll it up and place it into a baking dish. Repeat the process to fill the baking dish.
6. Spread the remainder of the sauce and cheese over the enchiladas. Bake at 350 degrees for 10-12 minutes or until the cheese is nice and melted.

NOTE:
FRYING THE TORTILLA KEEPS IT FROM FALLING APART OR GETTING DRY.

RED CHILAQUILES

By Salty Cocina

INGREDIENTS

- 2 ROMA TOMATOES
- 4-5 CHILE GUAJILLOS
- 3-4 CHILES DE ARBOL (OPTIONAL)
- 2 GARLIC CLOVES
- 1 TBSP CHICKEN OR TOMATO BOUILLON
- 1/2 TSP CUMIN
- 1 TSP OREGANO
- VEGETABLE OIL
- 12-15 TORTILLAS

TOPPING SUGGESTIONS:
Cilantro, Onions, Queso Cotija, Queso Fresco Sour Cream, Avocado, Fried Egg

PREPARATION: 10MIN
COOKING: 20 MIN
READY IN: 30MIN

INSTRUCTIONS

1. Remove the stems and seeds from the chile guajillo.
2. Boil the guajillo, Chile de Arbol, and the tomatoes for 5 minutes.
3. Blend the ingredients from the saucepan along with the garlic and oregano.
4. Heat a generous amount of oil, over med/high, add the tortillas, fry until golden brown. You can also use baked or store-bought corn tortilla chips.
5. Remove the fried tortillas and, using the same pan, add in the sauce. Add the remainder of the seasonings and simmer for 5 minutes before adding the fried tortillas. Move the tortillas around to ensure they are well coated with the sauce, serve them right away.
6. Top them off with your favorite toppings and enjoy with a fried egg or your favorite side.

AGUACHILE

Green Chile Lime Marinated Shrimp

By Salty Cocina

INGREDIENTS

- 2 LBS LARGE RAW SHRIMP PEELED AND
- DEVEINED
- ONE SMALL BUNDLE OF CILANTRO
- 3-4 TOMATILLOS
- 6-8 LIMES (1 - 1/2 CUPS)
- SALT & PEPPER
- 2 TBSP VINEGAR
- 1 LARGE CUCUMBER
- 1 SMALL RED ONION

PREP TIME: 25 MIN
COOK TIME: 1 HR

INSTRUCTIONS

1. Clean the shrimp, cut it in half, and season with salt and pepper.
2. Arrange the shrimp in a large baking dish
3. Blend the cilantro, serrano peppers, tomatillos, vinegar, and lime juice
4. Pour the chili-lime sauce over the shrimp, making sure it's completely submerged in the sauce
5. Thinly slice the cucumber and the red onion and arrange them over the shrimp
6. Sprinkle with chile flakes
7. Cover and refrigerate for 1 hour
8. Serve on tostadas or chips, garnish with slices of avocado and drizzle with your favorite salsa.

SHRIMP COCKTAIL

By Salty Cocina

INGREDIENTS

- 2 LBS LARGE SHRIMP PEELED AND DEVEINED
- 4 CUPS WATER
- 2 GARLIC CLOVES
- 1/4 WHITE ONION
- 2 BAY LEAVES
- 2 LARGE CUCUMBERS
- 2-3 LIMES
- 2 -3 LARGE AVOCADOS
- 1-2 SERRANO PEPPERS (OPTIONAL)

- 1/4 RED ONION
- HALF A BUNDLE OF CILANTRO
- SALT & PEPPER ONE
- 32 OZ BOTTLE OF YOUR FAVORITE TOMATO COCKTAIL OR VEGETABLE V8
- 1 CUP KETCHUP
- 1/4 CUP CHIPOTLE ADOBO SAUCE

INSTRUCTIONS

- Boil two pounds of peeled and deveined shrimp in four cups of water, 1/4 onion, two garlic cloves, and one bay leaf for 3-4 minutes or until they reach a pink/salmon color.
- Drain out the water and place the shrimp in cold water or an ice bath to stop the cooking process.
- Dice the cucumbers, avocados, serrano peppers, red onion, and cilantro.
- Mix the ketchup, chipotle adobo sauce, lime juice, and V8 Juice or tomato cocktail mix in a large bowl.
- Mix in the cooled shrimp and the vegetables.
- Season with salt and pepper to your taste.
- Enjoy right away or, for best results, refrigerate for one hour.
- Serve with saltine crackers and your favorite beverage!
- For a more accessible version, use precooked shrimp. You can adjust the number of vegetables used to your taste.

PREPARATION: 30 MIN
COOKING: 5 MIN
READY IN: 35 MIN
MAKES 4-5 LARGE COCKTAILS

STUFFED CHILAQUILES

By Salty Cocina

INGREDIENTS

- 10-12 TOMATILLOS
- 2-3 JALAPEÑOS (MORE FOR EXTRA SPICY) 2 GARLIC CLOVES
- 1/2 MEDIUM WHITE ONION EPAZOTE OR CILANTRO
- 1 TBSP CHICKEN BOUILLON
- 1 CUP CHICKEN BROTH OR WATER

MASA INGREDIENTS

- 2 CUPS CORN FLOUR
- 1/2 TSP SALT
- 1-3/4 -2 CUPS VERY WARM WATER AVOCADO OIL FOR FRYING
- MOZZARELLA CHEESE OR YOUR FAVORITE MELTING CHEESE

TOPPING SUGGESTIONS:
CILANTRO, RED ONION, QUESO FRESCO, AND OR
CREMA MEXICANA OR SOUR CREAM

INSTRUCTIONS

1. Boil the tomatillos and the jalapeños over medium heat for five minutes or until they turn a pale green color.
2. *Blend the tomatillos, jalapeños, garlic, onion with the chicken broth or water.*
3. *In a medium saucepan, heat a small amount of vegetable oil and add the blender's contents. Bring to a simmer and simmer for five minutes over medium heat. Season the sauce with chicken bouillon or salt and a sprig of epazote or cilantro.*
4. *Prepare the masa by mixing the masa, salt, and warm water. Mix for 5 minutes or until smooth.*
5. Shape a one-inch round, and using a tortilla press, place the dough between two pieces of plastic and shape it into a five-inch round. Remove the top plastic, add cheese to one side of the uncooked tortilla, fold over the second half and pinch close the edges. Cut folded tortilla in half to form two triangular shapes and pinch seal the edges of the cut.
6. *Preheat your preferred oil and fry until golden on both sides.*
7. *Smothered with the green sauce, serve right away with favorite topping.*

PREP TIME: 30
COOK TIME: 15
TOTAL TIME: 45
4-5 SERVINGS AS
PICTURED

TAMARIND SHRIMP KABOBS

By Salty Cocina

INGREDIENTS

- 2 LBS LARGE SHRIMP PEELED & DEVEINED SALT & PEPPER
- 1 CUP (2 -3 OZ) TAMARINDO PASTE
- 1 CUP WATER
- 2 HABANERO PEPPERS 1 LARGE GARLIC CLOVE
- 1/2 CUP ORANGE JUICE 1/3 CUP OLIVE OIL

- 2 TBSP VINEGAR
- TWO ZUCCHINI
- 1 PINEAPPLE
- 2 BELL PEPPERS OF YOUR CHOICE
- ONE RED ONION

MAKES 12-15 KABOBS

INSTRUCTIONS

1. Over medium heat, break down the tamarindo paste in one cup of water until you have thick and paste.
2. Blend the habaneros, garlic, orange juice, olive oil, and vinegar
3. Mix the ingredients from the blender with half of the tamarind paste.
4. Season the shrimp with salt and add the marinade from the blender; cover and refrigerate for one hour.
5. Meanwhile, dice the zucchini, pineapple, and bell peppers
6. Thread the skewers with the shrimp, vegetables, and pineapple
7. Grill for 2-3 minutes on each side. Baste with the remainder of the tamarindo paste while grilling
8. Enjoy!

GORDITAS

Stuffed with Chicharron

By Salty Cocina

CHICHARRON INGREDIENTS

- 4-5 CUPS OF CHICHARRON OR PORK RINDS
- 3 ROMA TOMATOES
- 4 CHILE GUAJILLO
- 5-6 CHILES DE ARBOL FOR SPICE
- 3 GARLIC CLOVES
- 1- 1 1/2 CUPS WATER
- 1 TSP OREGANO
- 1/2 TSP CUMIN SALT TO YOUR TASTE

Topping Suggestions

Cilantro, queso fresco or queso cotija, salsa or pico de gallo

INSTRUCTIONS

1. Break down four cups of pork rinds or chicharron by hand or in a food processor.
2. Over medium heat, roast the tomatoes, peppers, and garlic for 10-12 minutes with frequent movement. Remove the garlic after one minute, so it doesn't burn.
3. Blend the roasted tomatoes, peppers, and garlic with one cup of water
4. Roughly chop 1/2 medium onion and saute in a small amount of oi for one minute.
5. Add in the sauce from the blender and season with oregano, cumin, and salt to your taste.
6. Simmer for 2-3 minutes over low/med heat, then mix in the pork rinds and simmer for an additional five minutes or until most of the sauce has simmered down and the pork rinds are pliable.

INSTRUCTIONS

GORDITA INGREDIENTS

- 2 CUPS CORN FLOUR
- 3/4 CUP FLOUR
- 1 TSP SALT
- 1-1/2 CUPS WARM WATER OR
  AS NEEDED

1. In a medium bowl combine the cornflour, flour, and salt.
2. Mix in one cup of warm water and continue adding the remainder of the water a little at a time. Mix until the masa comes together until it no longer sticks to the side of the bowl or your hands.
3. Shape the masa into two-inch rounds and cover with a clean kitchen towel or plastic wrap to keep them from getting dry.
4. Shape the gorditas by hand or with a tortilla press into 4-5 inch rounds and about 1/4 of an inch thick.
5. Preheat your griddle or pan to low/med heat and cook the gordita for about 1-2 minutes on each side.
6. Using a small paring knife, cut a slit down the edge of one side. The gordita should open into a cute little pocket to stuff with a filling of your choice.
7. Enjoy with your favorite topping and salsa

CHICHARONES RANCHEROS

By Salty Cocina

INGREDIENTS

- 4 MEDIUM CACTUS PADS
- 1 MEDIUM WHITE ONION (DIVIDED)
- 4-5 TOMATILLOS
- 1 ROMA TOMATO
- 4-5 SERRANO PEPPERS
- 2-3 GARLIC CLOVES
- 2 CUPS WATER
- 1/2 TSP CUMIN
- 1/2 TSP SALT
- 1 TBSP MEXICAN OREGANO
- 1 TBSP CHICKEN BOUILLON
- 4-5 CUPS OF HOMEMADE OR STORE-BOUGHT PORK RINDS OR CHICHARRON
- 2-3 TBSP VEGETABLE OIL
- JUICE FOR 1/2 LIME

INSTRUCTIONS

1. Roast the tomatillos, peppers, 3/4 onion, and garlic over medium heat for 8-10 minutes (remove the onion and garlic after 1-2 minutes)
2. Clean and dice the cactus pads
3. In a medium pan, heat your vegetable oil, add the diced cactus, 1/4 of the onion roughly chopped, 1 tsp of salt, and lime juice to reduce the slime. Cook 15-20 minutes or until the slime is minimal or none.
4. Blend the roasted ingredients in two cups of water and seasonings and pour it into the pan with the cactus.
5. Bring to a simmer, add in the pork rinds or chicharron and simmer over low-medium heat for 8-10 minutes or until the pork rinds are pliable.
6. Simmer over low, medium heat for 8-10 minutes or until the pork rinds are pliable.
7. Cover for 10 minutes and enjoy with your favorite sides or in a taco!

PREPARATION: 10MIN
COOKING: 30 MIN
READY IN: 40 MIN

PICKLED PIG FEET

By Salty Cocina

INGREDIENTS

- 3-4 LBS OF PIG FEET CUT IN HALF
- 8-10 CUPS OF WATER
- 1 TBSP SALT
- 3 TBSP MEXICAN OREGANO
- 1 WHITE ONION (DIVIDED)
- 3 CUPS OF WHITE VINEGAR (DIVIDED)
- 3 BAY LEAVES
- 3 LARGE CARROTS
- 2-3 JALAPEÑOS
- 2 TBSP SALT
- 28 OZ CAN OF PICKLED JALAPEÑOS

INSTRUCTIONS

1. Rinse the pig feet
2. Fill a large stockpot with water and add the salt, peppercorns, 2 tbsp Mexican oregano, bay leaves, 1/2 white onion, the pig feet, and the vinegar.
3. Bring to a boil over medium-high heat. Once it reaches a boiling point, turn down the burner to low heat, cover, and boil for 2 to 2 1/2 hrs.
4. Dice the carrots, the other half of the onion, and jalapeños into rounds.
5. In a separate skillet, heat up the vegetable oil add the onion, jalapeños, and carrots. Season with the remainder of the Mexican oregano, black pepper, and saute for 5-7 minutes over medium heat.
6. Add the pig feet into a glass jar or container large enough to accommodate all the ingredients. Add the vegetables from the skillet, the can of pickled jalapeños, 1 Tbsp salt, the remainder of the vinegar, and 1-1/2 cups of water.
7. Cover for 3-4 hours
8. Drizzle with fresh lime juice to bring out the flavor before enjoying.

CHILES EN NOGADA

By Salty Cocina

INGREDIENTS

- 6-8 CHILES POBLANOS
- 1/2 LB LEAN GROUND BEEF
- 1/2 LB GROUND PORK
- 1 ROMA TOMATO
- 1/2 MEDIUM WHITE ONION
- ONE PEACH
- ONE SWEET APPLE
- 1 PLANTAIN
- 1 PEAR
- 1/2 CUP RAISINS
- 1/2 CUP CHOPPED ALMONDS
- 1/4 TSP GROUND CLOVES
- 1/4 TSP CUMIN
- 1/2 TSP CINNAMON
- 1/2 TSP SALT
- 1/4 CUP COOKING SHERRY
- 1/2 CUP CANDIED CACTUS, CITRON, PINEAPPLE,OR MANGO BITS

PREP TIME: TIME: 30 MINUTES
COOK TIME: 30 MINUTES
TOTAL TIME: 1 HRS
5-6 SERVINGS

WALNUT SAUCE INGREDIENTS

- 1 CUP OF WALNUTS
- 2 CUPS OF WHOLE MILK
- 8 OZ CREAM CHEESE
- 4 OZ GOAT CHEESE
- 1/2 CUP SOUR CREAM
- 1 TSP CINNAMON
- 1 TBSP SUGAR

GARNISH WITH POMEGRANATE SEEDS AND PARSLEY

INSTRUCTIONS

1. Roast the Poblano Peppers over an open flame, in the oven, air fryer, or on a griddle for 12-15 minutes. Transfer them to a plastic bag for 15-20 minutes. Doing so will loosen up the skin, and it will make it much easier to peel. Remove the skin, make a small incision on the side of the pepper, and remove the seeds.
2. Soak the walnuts in 2 cups of milk
3. Dice the apple, pear, peach, and plantain into small bite-size pieces
4. Over medium-high heat, brown the ground beef and pork for 12-15 minutes and season with salt, cumin, cloves, and cinnamon.
5. In a separate pan, lightly fry the plantain for 1-2 minutes or until golden.
6. Add in half a minced onion, one Roma tomato, and cook for an additional 4-5 minutes.
7. Mix in the chopped almonds, raisins, and sherry, cook for an additional 2-3 minutes with frequent movement.
8. Add in the diced fruit one at a time stirring for 30 seconds to 1 minute in between. Mix in the plantains last
9. Fill the peppers with the picadillo.
10. Prepare the walnut sauce by mixing the walnuts with the milk, cream cheese, goat cheese, sour cream, cinnamon, and sugar. If needed, add more milk to adjust the thickness.
11. Plate over a bed of the walnut sauce and top off with more sauce
12. Garnish with minced parsley and pomegranate seeds.

RED PORK POZOLE

By Salty Cocina

INGREDIENTS

- 7-8 LBS OF BONE-IN PORK SHOULDER OR PORK BUTT OR BONE-IN CHICKEN BREASTS
- 4-5 QUARTS OF WATER
- 2 TBSP SALT
- 2-3 BAY LEAVES
- 1 LARGE WHITE ONION
- 1 HEAD OF GARLIC
- 20 CHILE GUAJILLO, CALIFORNIA OR NM CHILI PODS
- 2 CHILE ANCHOS
- 6-8 CHILES DE ARBOL FOR SPICE
- 2 TBSP MEXICAN OREGANO 1
- 1/2 TBSP GROUND CUMIN
- 3-4 TBSP CHICKEN OR BEEF BOUILLON
- 6 LBS OR HOMINY (ONE LARGE CAN)

TOPPING SUGGESTIONS
CABBAGE OR LETTUCE, ONIONS, CHILI FLAKES,
OREGANO, LIME JUICE, RADISHES, CHIPS

INSTRUCTIONS

1. Rinse the meat, cut it into 3-4 inch pieces, and trim off as much meat from the bone as possible.
2. Fill a large stockpot with 4-5 quarts of water, add in the meat, one onion cut in half, one entire head of garlic, bay leaves, and 2 tbsp of salt. Boil for one hour to an hour and a half.
3. Remove the seeds and stem from the guajillo and chile anchos. Soak them in hot water for10-15 minutes or until pliable.
4. Fish out the onion and garlic from the stockpot, carefully add in the hominy.
5. Blend the peppers with the onion, garlic, and 2 cups of water from the same stockpot. (squeeze out the garlic from the husk by pressing with a knife before adding it to the blender)
6. Strain the sauce into the stockpot and add the remainder of the seasonings, salt, or chicken or beef bouillon.
7. Boil on medium heat for an additional 30 minutes.
8. Enjoy with your favorite toppings!

PREP TIME: TIME: 30 MINUTES
COOK TIME: 2 HRS MINUTES
TOTAL TIME: 2 1/2 TO 3 HOURS
10-12 SERVINGS

CARNE EN SU JUGO

By Salty Cocina

INGREDIENTS

- 1-1/2 - 2 LBS CHUCK ROAST - FLANK STEAK
- 1/4 CUP VEGETABLE OR OLIVE OIL
- 10-12 OZ PACKAGE OF BACON
- 2 BUNDLES OF CAMBRAY/SPRING ONIONS
- 1 LB TOMATILLOS
- 3-4 SERRANO OR JALAPEÑOS

- HALF WHITE ONION DIVIDED
- 1-2 TBSP CHICKEN OR BEEF BOUILLON
- BLACK PEPPER
- 2-3 GARLIC CLOVES
- HANDFUL OF CILANTRO
- 3-4 CUPS BEEF BROTH
- CANNED OR FRESH PINTO BEANS

PREP TIME: TIME: 30 MINUTES
COOK TIME: 1 HR 15 MINUTES
TOTAL TIME: 2 HRS
16-8 SERVINGS

TOPPING SUGGESTIONS:
CILANTRO, ONIONS, BACON,
RADISHES, LIME JUICE

INSTRUCTIONS

1. Cut the meat into two- three-inch strips.
2. Pour the oil over the meat, generously season with salt and pepper, and set aside for about 15 minutes.
3. Remove the husk from the tomatillos and rinse them; Boil the tomatillos, jalapenos, or serrano peppers in 4 cups of water for 5 minutes or until they turn a pale green color. Drain out the water and blend them with 1/4 onion, garlic, cilantro, and one cup of beef broth or water
4. Trim the tips of the spring onions, leaving them to about 6-7 inches in length.
5. Cut the bacon into small bits and fry it in a dutch oven over medium-high heat with frequent movement until crispy. Remove the bacon and use the same grease rendered from the bacon; fry the Cambray or spring onions for 2-3 minutes, remove them and set them aside with the bacon.
6. Remove some of the excess bacon fat if needed, add in the meat, cover, and cook over medium heat for approximately 30 minutes; move it around every 10 minutes.
7. After 30 minutes, add the sauce from the blender with three additional cups of beef broth.
8. Bring to a simmer and add beef, chicken bouillon, or salt if needed,
9. Bring to a simmer, cover, and cook over low heat for an additional 30 minutes.
10. Add half of the bacon and the Cambray/spring onions and simmer for an additional 10-12 minutes.
11. Serve with canned or fresh pinto beans.

POZOLE BLANCO

By Salty Cocina

INGREDIENTS

- 3 LBS PORK SHOULDER OR CHICKEN BREAST
- 1/2 WHITE ONION
- 1 HEAD OF GARLIC
- 8-1 0 CUPS OF WATER
- 1 TBSP OF SALT OR AS NEEDED
- 6-8 ALLSPICE BERRIES
- 1 TBSP MEXICAN OREGANO
- 8-10 PEPPERCORNS
- TWO 30OZ CANS OF HOMINY

SUGGESTED TOPPINGS

CABBAGE, SERRANO PEPPERS, WHITE OR RED ONION, OREGANO, RADISHES, AVOCADO, CHILI FLAKES, LIMES
ENJOY WITH TOSTADAS, CHIPS, FRIED TAQUITOS, OR WARM CORN TORTILLAS.

INSTRUCTIONS

1. In a large stockpot, heat the water over high heat and bring it to a boil.
2. Cut the pork into 1-2 inch pieces.
3. Trim both ends of the garlic and remove the excess husks.
4. Add the pork, onion, garlic, and bay leaves to the stockpot and boils for 30 minutes.
5. Using a mortar with a pestle, grind the peppercorns and allspice berries and add them to the pot along with the salt. Turn down the burner to low, cover, and cook for an additional 30 minutes.
6. Drain out the liquid from the can of hominy and add it to the rest of the ingredients; cover and cook for an additional 20 minutes or until the meat is nice and tender.
7. Enjoy with your favorite topping!

PREPARATION: 30
COOKING: 1-1/2 HRS
READY IN: 2 HRS

CHICKEN STEW

By Salty Cocina

INGREDIENTS

- 6-7 CHICKEN THIGHS OR DRUMSTICKS
- 6 ROMA TOMATOES
- 3 CHILE GUAJILLO
- 1/2 WHITE ONION
- 3 GARLIC CLOVES
- 1 TSP PAPRIKA & GROUND CORIANDER
- 2 TBSP CHICKEN BOUILLON
- SALT & PEPPER
- 2 QUARTS OF WATER OF CHICKEN BROTH (8 CUPS)
- 1 CHAYOTE SQUASH OR 2 MEDIUM POTATOES
- 3 LARGE CARROTS, 3-4 EARS OR CORN & 1 CUP FRESH GREEN BEANS

INSTRUCTIONS

1. If using thighs, remove the skin and trim off the excess fat, and season front and back with salt and pepper.
2. In a medium saucepan, boil the tomatoes and guajillo peppers for 5-7 minutes.
3. Dice your vegetables into small bite-size pieces. Cut each ear of corn into four parts,
4. Heat a small amount of oil in a large stockpot and sear the chicken on both sides for 5-7 minutes over medium heat. Remove and set aside.
5. Blend the tomatoes, guajillo, onion, garlic, and seasoning with 2 cups of chicken broth or water.
6. Using the same pot, strain the sauce from the blender and bring it to a boil.
7. Add the chicken back into the pot along with the vegetables.
8. Boil on Low/med for 20-25 minutes.
9. Enjoy over red rice with a bit of lime juice.

PREPARATION: 10MIN
COOKING: 10MIN
READY IN: 20MIN

PICADILLO STEW

By Salty Cocina

INGREDIENTS

- 1-1/2 TO 2 LBS OF LEAN GROUND BEEF
- SALT & PEPPER
- 2 MINCED GARLIC CLOVES
- 1 LARGE WHITE ONION (DIVIDED)
- 2-3 NM CHILE PODS OR CHILE GUAJILLO
- 4 ROMA TOMATOES
- 2-3 TBSP BEEF OR CHICKEN BOUILLON
- 1 TBSP MEXICAN OREGANO
- 1 TSP CUMIN
- 1 TSP CORRIANDER SEEDS
- 4-5 CUPS OF WATER
- (DIVIDED) 2 MEDIUM RUSSET OR YUKON GOLD POTATOES
- 1 CUP DICED CARROTS
- 1 CUP DICED CELERY
- 1 CUP FRESH OR CANNED CORN

INSTRUCTIONS

1. Remove the seeds from the chile guajillos and soak them in boiling water for about 5-7 minutes or until they are nice a pliable.
2. Season the ground beef with salt and pepper and set aside while you dice your vegetables.
3. MInce 1/2 of the white onion and the garlic. Dice the carrots, celery, and potatoes into small bite-size pieces.
4. In a large stockpot, cook the meat for about 10-12 minutes or until you no longer see red. Drain out the excess fat if needed before adding the minced onion and the garlic. Add the onion and garlic and saute for five more minutes.
5. Mix in the diced potatoes, celery, corn and cook for about 1-2 minutes
6. Blend the chile guajillo, tomatoes, the other half of the onion, 2 cups of water, and the seasonings.
7. Bring to a boil over medium heat, and after 5 minutes, add in the diced zucchini. Mix in the sauce with the rest of the ingredients and an additional three cups of water. Season with chicken or beef bouillon as needed.
8. Simmer for an additional ten minutes and cover for ten to fifteen minutes before serving.
9. Serve over red rice, and enjoy!

PREP TIME: TIME: 20 MINUTES
COOK TIME: 30 MINUTES
TOTAL TIME: 50 MINUTES
10-12 SERVIINGS

CORN SOUP

By Salty Cocina

INGREDIENTS

- 5-6 WHOLE CORNS OF 3-4 CANS OF CORN
- 2 POBLANO PEPPERS
- 2 ROMA TOMATOES
- 1 JALAPEÑO (OPTIONAL)
- 1/2 MEDIUM WHITE ONION
- 2 STALKS OF CELERY
- 1 GARLIC CLOVE
- 3 TBSP BUTTER
- 1 TSP BASIL PASTE
- 1-1/2 CUPS HEAVY CREAM
- 5-6 CUPS OF WATER OR CHICKEN BROTH DIVIDED
- 2 TBSP CHICKEN BOUILLON
- 10OZ OF PANELA CHEESE

PREPARATION: 20MIN
COOKING: 15 MIN
READY IN: 35
6 SERVINGS

INSTRUCTIONS

1. Roast the poblano peppers, place them in a bag for 15 minutes, then peel them remove the seeds, and dice them into half-inch strips.
2. Remove the husk for the corn and, using a sharp knife, trim off the corn kernels, reserve one cup of the corn kernels in a separate bowl
3. dice the tomatoes, onion, celery, and finely mince the garlic.
4. In a stockpot, melt 3 tbsp of butter.
5. Add in the tomatoes, onion, and garlic and saute for 5 minutes.
6. mix in the corn and the celery
7. Blend the remainder of the corn kernels with heavy cream, sour cream, and 1 cup of water or broth.
8. Add 5 cups of water to the stockpot and immediately add the ingredients from the blender before it gets too hot. Bring to a simmer and simmer over medium heat for 10-12 minutes.
9. Dice the panela cheese into small bite-size pieces and add it to the stockpot and simmer for an additional 2-3 minutes.
10. Turn off the burner and cover for 10-15 minutes before serving.

BEEF TAMALES

By Salty Cocina

INGREDIENTS

- 7-8 LBS BEEF, CHICKEN, OR PORK
- 1 LARGE WHITE ONION 1
- HEAD OF GARLIC
- 3 BAY LEAVES
- BEEF OR CHICKEN BOUILLON (5-6 TBSP) SALT (3-4 TBSP)
- 5 LBS OF CORN FLOUR
- 1-1/2 TO 2 LBS OF LARD OR 3-4 CUPS OF VEGETABLE, CANOLA, OR OLIVE OIL
- 1 TBSP CUMIN
- 20 CHILE GUAJILLO OR NM OR CALIFORNIA CHILI PODS
- 20 CHILE GUAJILLO OR NM OR CALIFORNIA CHILI PODS
- 3 CHILE ANCHOS
- 10 CHILES DE ARBOL (OPTIONAL)
- BEEF BROTH 10-14 CUPS
- 14-15 CUPS OF WATER TO BOIL THE MEAT
- 60-70 CORN HUSKS

PREPARATION: 4-1/2 HRS
COOKING: 3 HRS
READY IN: 7-1/2 HRS

Note: Substitute one cup of oil for every 1/2 lb of lard. If using oil, the amount of broth needed may be less. It's always best to keep the extra canned broth in case it is required or enough broth renders from the meat.

INSTRUCTIONS

1. Cut 7-8 lbs boneless chuck roast or brisket into 3 to 4-inch pieces.
2. To a large stockpot, add 14-15 cups of water, the onion cut in half, the entire head of garlic, three bay leaves, 3 tbsps of beef bouillon, 1 tbsp of salt, and the meat.
3. Boil for 2 to 2 1/2 hrs.
4. Soak 70-80 corn husk in hot water for 2-3 hours.
5. Remove the stems and seed from the guajillo and the chile anchos. Add chiles de arbol to add extra heat; no need to remove the seeds. Rinse the peppers.
6. Remove the onion and the garlic from the stockpot and transfer the meat to a different stockpot, but not discard the broth.
7. Soak the peppers in the hot broth for 12-15 minutes or until pliable.
8. Chop the meat into small pieces and transfer it back into the same stockpot.
9. Transfer the peppers to the blender and blend with one tbsp of cumin, two cups of water or broth, and the onion and garlic retrieved from the stockpot. Blend until smooth.
10. Mix 3/4 of the sauce from the blender with the meat. Season with salt or beef bouillon and adjust the thickness with beef broth if needed.
11. Strain the broth from the stockpot.
12. Add 5 lbs of cornflour to a large bowl and mix in 2 tbsp of baking powder and 2 tbsp of salt.
13. Mix in two lbs of lard until it reaches a crumbly texture.
14. Add the remainder of the sauce to the blender. Add 2-3 cups of broth to the blender, cover, give it a good shake, and add the cornflour. Using a wooden spoon, mix the masa and add broth until you have a smooth, fluffy masa. Mixing time should be about 20-30 minutes. For the 5 lbs of cornflour, I used a total of 14 cups of broth.
15. Remove the corn husks and pat them dry.
16. Using a spatula, spread 2-3 tbsp of masa on the bottom portion of the corn husk and add a couple of tbsp of meat right in the middle of the masa. Fold over the first flap and overlap the second flap. Fold over the tip and set it on a cookie sheet. Continue with the rest until you run out of meat and masa.
17. Fill the steamer with 4-5 cups of water or enough to not go past the liner.
18. Arrange the tamales with the flap facing the wall of the steamer. Begin on the outer edge and work your way into the middle.
19. Cover the tamales with husks or a clean kitchen towel to hold more of the steam.
20. Boil on low/med heat for 2-1/2 to 3 hours. Make sure to check the water level often. Add hot boiling water if needed.
21. Allow the tamales to cool down for 10 minutes before enjoying.

CREAMY CHICKEN ENCHILADAS

By Salty Cocina

INGREDIENTS

- 5-6 BONE-IN CHICKEN THIGHS
- BOIL WITH 1/4 ONION, CILANTRO, AND SALT
- 1/4 ONION MINCED
- 1 GARLIC CLOVE MINCED
- ONE 10 OZ CREAM OF CHICKEN
- 1 CUP CHICKEN BROTH
- 15-20 TORTILLAS
- CHEDDAR JACK CHEESE

SAUCE INGREDIENTS

- 8-10 TOMATILLOS
- 3-4 SERRANO OR JALAPEÑOS FOR EXTRA SPICE (OPTIONAL)
- 1 GARLIC CLOVE
- HANDFUL OF CILANTRO
- 4-5 ANAHEIM PEPPERS
- 2 CUPS OF CHICKEN BROTH
- 1-2 TBSP CHICKEN BOUILLON OR SALT

Topping suggestions: Lettuce, tomatoes, cilantro, queso fresco, queso cotija, mexican sour cream, avocado

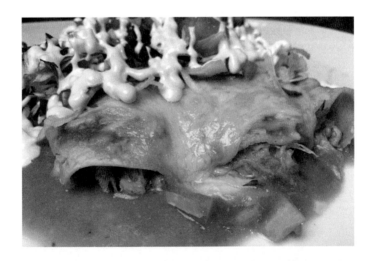

INSTRUCTIONS

1. Boil the chicken in 2 quarts of water, a small handful of cilantro, 1/4 of a white onion, and salt.
2. Shred the chicken and reserved 2 cups of chicken broth.
3. Roast the anaheim peppers, peel them, and remove the stems and the seeds.
4. Boil the tomatillos and serranos for 5-7 minutes.
5. Blend the anaheim peppers, tomatillos, serranos, garlic, cilantro, and 2 cups of chicken broth from the chicken.
6. In a medium saucepan, heat a small amount of cooking oil, add the sauce and the remainder of the seasonings. Mix them in and simmer for 5 minutes over med heat.
7. In a medium saucepan, heat 2 tbsp of your preferred cooking oil, saute 1/4 of a minced onion and garlic clove for 1 minute and then mix in the shredded chicken.
8. Mix in the cream of chicken and simmer over med heat for 5-7 minutes.
9. Heat a generous amount of cooking oil in a separate pan and lightly fry each tortilla until pliable.
10. Spread a generous amount of enchilada sauce to the bottom of the baking dish.
11. To prepare your enchilada, add a spoonful of the chicken, a spoonful of cheese, roll them and place them in the baking dish with the flap down.
12. Spread the remainder of the sauce over the enchiladas and top them off with the rest of the cheese.
13. Bake at 350 degrees for 12-15 minutes or until the cheese is nice and melted.
14. Serve right away with your favorite side dish and toppings.
15. Enjoy!

PREPARATION: 30 MIN
COOKING: 20 MIN
READY IN: 50 MIN
SERVINGS 12-15

Tacos

STOVETOP TACOS AL PASTOR
Prepared with easy to find ingredients

By Salty Cocina

INGREDIENTS

- 4-5 LBS DICED PORK SHOULDER OR PORK BUTT
- 1 TBSP SALT
- 1 TSP BLACK PEPPER
- I CUP PINEAPPLE BITS
- 1 CUP ORANGE JUICE OR PINEAPPLE JUICE
- 1 MEDIUM WHITE ONION
- 5 CHILE GUAJILLOS
- 1 OZ ACHIOTE PASTE
- 1 TBSP OREGANO
- 1 TSP CUMIN
- 1 TSP GROUND CINNAMON
- 3-4 GARLIC CLOVES

INSTRUCTIONS

1. Remove the stems and seed from the chile guajillo and soak them in boiling water for 15 minutes.
2. Dice the meat into small one-inch pieces and transfer them to a bowl.
3. Blend the guajillo peppers and orange juice, achiote paste, garlic, cinnamon, cumin, and oregano.
4. Season the meat with salt and pepper.
5. Mix in the chopped onion, pineapple bits, and the sauce from the blender, cover, and refrigerate for 4-5 hrs or overnight.
6. Cook all the ingredients in a heavy bottom pan until all the liquid has simmered down.
7. Use the meat to make tacos or nacho topping!

PREPARATION: 4 HRS
COOKING: 30 MIN
READY IN: 4-5 HRS

SHREDDED
BEEF TACOS

SHREDDED BEEF TACOS

By Salty Cocina

INGREDIENTS

- 5LBS BONELESS CHUCK-ROAST
- 2 TBSP NM CHILI POWDER
- 2 MEDIUM TOMATOES
- 1/2 LARGE ONION
- 3 GARLIC CLOVES
- 2 JALAPEÑOS (OPTIONAL)
- 1 TBSP MEXICAN OREGANO
- 1 TSP GROUND CORRIANDER
- 1 TSP GROUND ALLSPICE
- 1 TSP CUMIN
- SALT & PEPPER
- 2 CUPS BEEF BROTH
- 1-1/2 CUPS ORANGE JUICE

PICO DE GALLO INGREDIENTS

- TWO SERRANO OR JALAPEÑO PEPPERS
- TWO ROMA TOMATOES
- 1/2 MEDIUM WHITE OR RED ONION
- A SMALL HANDFUL OF CILANTRO
- SALT & PEPPER

INSTRUCTIONS

1. Cut the meat into 3-4 inch pieces and generously season with salt and pepper
2. Finely mince the tomatoes, jalapeños, onion, and garlic.
3. Melt 2-3 Tbsp of lard or vegetable oil and sear the beef a few pieces at a time.
4. Using the same pot, add in the minced vegetable and saute for about 2-3 minutes
5. Add in the chili powder, allspice, oregano, cumin, beef broth, and orange juice.
6. Add the meat back into the pot; once it reaches a light simmer, turn down the burner to low heat, cover, and cook for 2 1/2 - 3 hours.

Serve on corn or flour tortillas.

STOVETOP BEEF BIRRIA

By Salty Cocina

INGREDIENTS

- 5-7 LBS OF BONELESS CHUCK ROAST
- 1 MEDIUM WHITE ONION
- I HEAD OF GARLIC
- 1-2 TBSP SALT
- 2-3 BAYS LEAVES
- 10-12 CHILE GUAJILLO, NM OR CALIFORNIA CHILE PODS
- 3 CHILE ANCHOS
- 6-8 CHILES DE ARBOL
- 6-8 PEPPERCORNS
- 4-5 WHOLE CLOVES
- 1 TBSP MEXICAN OREGANO
- 1/2 GROUND CORIANDER
- 1 TSP CUMIN
- BEEF BOUILLON AS NEEDED (2-3 TBSP)
- 8- 10 CUPS OF WATER
- 2 CUPS OF BEEF BROTH

OTHER INGREDIENTS NEEDED

mince onion, cilantro, radishes
corn tortillas,
your favorite melting cheese
(mozzarella, pepper jack, Oaxaca cheese, cheddar jack, etc.)
Salsa

INSTRUCTIONS

1. Cut the meat into 3-4 inch pieces and generously season with salt and pepper.
2. In a large stockpot, melt a tbsp of lard or cooking oil and sear the meat a few pieces at a time.
3. Heat a small amount of your preferred cooking oil in a large skillet and lightly toast the peppers, onion, and garlic over low, medium heat for about 1-2 minutes. Move them frequently, so they don't burn. If they burn, the sauce will have a bitter taste, and you will need to start over.
4. Remove the pan with the peppers from the burner and add 2 cups of beef broth. Soak for 10-15 minutes or until the peppers are nice and pliable.
5. Using a mortar, break down the peppercorns and the cloves.
6. Transfer the peppers to the blender along with the beef broth.
7. Strain the sauce into the pot and add the remainder of the seasonings.
8. Taste the broth before adding the beef bouillon and add as needed.
9. Once it reaches a light simmer, turn down the burner to low heat, and cover for 2-1/2 to 3 hours or until the meat is tender and falling apart.
10. Enjoy as a stew and top with minced cilantro, onion, and radishes.
11. Prepare birria queso tacos by dipping the cold tortilla in the broth, placing it on a preheated griddle, add cheese, cilantro, onion, and shredded birria meat. Cook for 1-2 minutes on each side over low heat or until the tortilla is lightly toasted.
12. ENJOY

PREP TIME: 30 MINUTES
COOK TIME: 2-1/2 TO 3 HRS
TOTAL TIME: 4 HRS 15-20
MAKES 8-10 SERVING (MORE IF MAKING BIRRIA TACOS)

SHREDDED CHICKEN TACOS

By Salty Cocina

INGREDIENTS

- 3-4 BONELESS CHICKEN BREAST
- 1/2 MEDIUM WHITE ONION
- 3 LARGE GARLIC CLOVES
- 4 ROMA TOMATOES
- 3-4 CHILE GUAJILLO, NM, CALIFORNIA CHILI PODS
- 4-5 CHILES DE ARBOL
- THREE DRY CHIPOTLE PEPPERS
- 1/2 TSP CUMIN
- 1/2 TSP OREGANO
- 1/2 TSP SALT & PEPPER
- 3 CUPS CHICKEN BROTH
- VEGETABLE SHORTENING
- CORN OR FLOUR TORTILLAS

TOPPING SUGGESTIONS

AVOCADO, CILANTRO, RED ONION, RADISHES, AND SALSA

PREP TIME: TIME: 30 MINUTES
COOK TIME: 30 MINUTES
 TOTAL TIME: 1 HRS
5-6 SERVINGS

SHREDDED CHICKEN TACOS

INSTRUCTIONS

- Remove the seeds and vines from the guajillo and chipotle peppers. (you can substitute the dry chipotle peppers for canned chipotle peppers)
- Mince the onion and the garlic
- In a medium saucepan, lightly fry the peppers for 1-2 minutes or until fragrant. Turn off the burner and add 2 cups of chicken broth. Soak for 10-15 minutes.
- Season the chicken breast front and back with salt and pepper
- Blend the cooled peppers and the rest of the ingredients, including the broth, and set aside.
- Using a dutch oven or heavy bottom pan, heat 2-3 Tbsp of your preferred cooking oil.
- Sear each chicken breast for 2-3 minutes on each side and remove it from the pan.
- Using the same pot, saute the minced onion and the garlic for 1-2 minutes.
- Add the sauce from the blender and bring to a simmer
- Add the chicken breasts back into the pot, turn down the burner to low heat, and cook for 30 minutes with the lid.
- Remove the chicken, and using two forks, shred the chicken.
- Add the shredded chicken back into the pot and simmer on low heat until most of the sauce simmers down.
- Serve on corn or flour tortillas.

STOVETOP CARNITAS

By Salty Cocina

INGREDIENTS

- 5-7 LBS PORK BUTT OR SHOULDER
- 1/2 LB LARD
- 2 TBSP BLACK PEPPER
- 2 TBSP SALT
- 1 TBSP CUMIN
- 5-6 LARGE GARLIC CLOVES

- MEDIUM WHITE ONION
- 12 OZ CAN DR. PEPPER OR COKE (NOT DIET)
- 1 CUP FRESH SQUEEZED ORANGE JUICE
- 6 OZ OF MEXICAN BEER (OPTIONAL)

INSTRUCTIONS

1. Dice 5-7 Lbs of pork butt or pork shoulder into 3-4 inch pieces.
2. Season with salt, pepper, and. Cumin.
3. In a large dutch oven pan or heavy bottom pan, melt the lard over medium-high heat, then add in the seasoned meat and sear the meat for about 10-12 minutes.
4. Add in the mince the garlic and the onion and cook for an additional five minutes before adding the coke, orange juice, lime juice, and beer.
5. Turn down the burner to low and cook for 2 - 2/1/2 hours, stirring once every 1/2 hr or so.
6. .Crisp up the meat in a cast iron or nonstick skillet, then serve on tacos, gorditas, burritos, or enjoy with your favorite sides.

Salsas

SALSA TAQUERA

By Salty Cocina

INGREDIENTS

- 8–10 TOMATILLO
- 10–12 CHILES DE ARBOL
- 3 GUAJILLO PEPPERS
- 1/2 MEDIUM WHITE ONION
- 1/2 BUNDLE OF CILANTRO
- 3 GARLIC CLOVES
- 1/2 TBSP SALT OR TO YOUR LIKING
- 1/2 CUP WATER

PREPARATION: 15 MIN
COOKING: 10 MIN
READY IN: 25 MIN

INSTRUCTIONS

1. Remove the husk from the tomatillos, remove the stem and the seed from the chile guajillo. Rinse the guajillo, chiles de arbol and tomatillos and pat them dry.
2. Finely chop the onion and the cilantro.
3. Heat a skillet over medium heat and roast the tomatillos unit blistered, and they have a pale green color.
4. Lightly toast the guajillo peppers, chiles de Arbol, and garlic for 30 seconds. Make sure to move them around frequently, so they don't burn; otherwise, you will have a bitter sauce.
5. Blend the peppers and the garlic with 1/2 cup of water until they smooth.   Add in the tomatillos and salt and blend for a few seconds.
6. Transfer to your salsa bowl and mix in the chopped onion and cilantro.
7. Enjoy with your favorite dishes or tacos!

Note: Adjust the spice level by adjusting the amount of chiles de arbol

ROASTED TOMATILLO SALSA

By Salty Cocina

INGREDIENTS

- 5-6 SERRANO PEPPERS
- 8-10 TOMATILLOS
- 1/2 MEDIUM ONION
- 2 LARGE GARLIC CLOVES
- 1 TSP SALT

PREP TIME: 5 COOK TIME: 20 TOTAL TIME: 25 SERVINGS: 2 CUPS

DIRECTIONS

1. Remove the husk from the tomatillos and rinse them well.
2. Remove the stems from the serrano peppers
3. Peel the garlic and cut the half onion in half
4. Roast all the ingredients over medium heat for 8-10 minutes or until charred and blistered. (remove the onion and the garlic after 1-2 minutes)
5. Once they cool down, blend the ingredients with 1 tsp of salt
6. Serve with your favorite dishes or tacos

SALSA MACHA

By Salty Cocina

INGREDIENTS

- 3/4 CUP OLIVE, AVOCADO, GRAPESEED, OR VEGETABLE OIL
- 1 CUP CHILE DE ARBOL
- 1 CUP JAPANESE PEPPERS
- 6-7 LARGE GARLIC CLOVES
- 1 CHILE GUAJILLO
- 1 TBSP CHILI POWDER
- SALT TO YOUR TASTE
- 1/4 CUP TOASTED PEANUTS (OPTIONAL)

Makes approximately one cup of salsa. This salsa is very spicy, a small amount goes a long way! Enjoy on eggs, chilaquiles, and especially birria tacos!

INSTRUCTIONS

1. Remove the stems of the chiles de Arbol. Removal of the seeds is not necessary but optional.
2. Blend the peppers in a blender or food choppers until they are well broken down and resemble chili flakes.
3. Peel and finely mince your garlic
4. If adding peanuts, lightly toast them and grind them in a mortar food processor.
5. In a small pan, heat the oil until it's close to boiling.
6. Remove from the burner and add in the chili flakes. Wait about 15-20 seconds before adding the garlic, chili powder, and salt.
7. Continue mixing until the oil cools down, add in the peanuts and transfer to a small dish.

PICO DE GALLO
2 WAYS

By Salty Cocina

INGREDIENTS

- I LARGE TOMATO DIVIDED OR 2 ROMA TOMATOES
- 1/2 WHITE ONION DIVIDED
- 2 JALAPEÑOS (DIVIDED)
- 1/2 BUNDLE OF CILANTRO
- SALT & PEPPER
- 1 AVOCADO

PREPARATION: 10 MIN
READY IN: 10 MIN

INSTRUCTIONS

1. Dice the tomato, onion, jalapeño, and cilantro and divide it evenly into two small bowls.
2. Dice the avocado and add it to one of the bowls. The avocado should not be overripe; otherwise, you will end up with guacamole.
3. Season with salt and pepper to your taste and mix in the seasonings.
4. Enjoy on tacos or with any of your favorite dishes,

CREAMY AVOCADO SALSA

By Salty Cocina

INGREDIENTS

- 3-4 SERRANO PEPPERS OR JALAPENOS
- 8-10 TOMATILLOS
- 1/4 ONION
- SMALL HANDFUL OF CILANTRO
- 2 GARLIC CLOVE
- 1 TSP SALT OR TO YOUR LIKING
- 1 LIME (1/3 CUP LIME JUICE) 1 LARGE RIPE AVOCADO

PREPARATION: 5 MIN
COOKING: 10 MIN
READY IN: 15 MIN

INSTRUCTIONS

1. Remove the husk from the tomatillos.
2. Boil the tomatillos and the serrano peppers for 5 minutes or until they turn a pale green color.
3. Blend the tomatillos, serranos, onion, garlic, salt, cilantro, and lime juice until it has a creamy texture.
4. Transfer the salsa to your favorite salsa dish or into a clear squeeze bottle.
5. Enjoy with your favorite tacos or dishes!

QUICK AND EASY RECIPES

BUTTERY FLOUR TORTILLAS

By Salty Cocina

INGREDIENTS

- 3 CUPS ALL-PURPOSE FLOUR
- 1 TSP SALT
- 1 TBSP BAKING POWDER
- 1/2 CUP SALTED OR UNSALTED BUTTER
- 1 CUP WATER
- EXTRA FLOUR FOR DUSTING

KITCHEN TOOLS

- ROLLING PIN
- GRIDDLE OR SKILLET
- KITCHEN TOWEL OR TORTILLA WARMER
- BOWL
- COOKIE SHEET

Makes 10-12 Tortillas
Prep Time 40 minutes
Cooking time 20 minutes

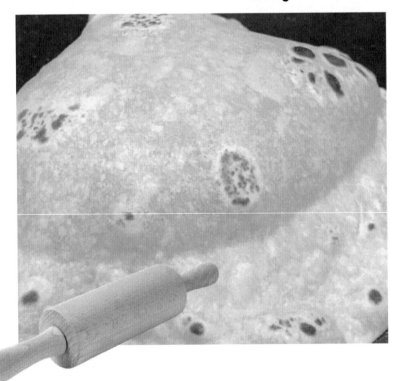

INSTRUCTIONS

1. Melt the butter in 1 cup of hot water.
2. In a medium bowl, combine the flour, salt, and baking powder.
3. Mix in the warm water with the rest of the ingredients.
4. Mix the dough until it comes together.
5. Transfer the dough onto a clean working surface and continue kneading for about five minutes or until the dough is nice and smooth.
6. Place the dough back into the bowl and cover with plastic for 10-15 minutes.
7. Shape the dough into equal-sized rounds (1-2 inches)
8. Arrange dough on a lightly floured cookie sheet and cover for ten more minutes
9. Preheat your skillet or griddle over medium heat
10. Using a rolling pin, shape the dough to a 10-12 inch round.
11. Place on the preheated skillet for approximately 10 seconds or until you see small bubbles form.
12. Flip and cook for an additional 15-20 seconds
13. Flip one last time and cook for 5-10 seconds or until your tortilla puffs up!
14. Place in a tortilla warmer or a kitchen towel to keep them warm and continue with the remaining.

To avoid your tortillas from getting hard; store them in a plastic bag while they are still warm. Refrigerate once they completely cool down; they stay fresh for up to a week.

CORN TORTILLAS

By Salty Cocina

INGREDIENTS

- 3 CUPS CORN FLOUR (MASECA)
- 1 TSP SALT
- 1-1/4 CUPS HOT WATER

KITCHEN TOOLS NEEDED

TORTILLA PRESS
2 PIECES OF PLASTIC, I USE A LARGE ZIPLOCK BACK CUT INTO 8- 10 INCH SQUARE
GRIDDLE, SKILLET, OR PAN

If you don't own a tortilla press, using two pieces of plastic, place the ball of dough between the two pieces of plastic, and using a heavy object, press down until you have 4-5 inches round.

NOTE: Prepared masa can be refrigerated and will stay fresh for up to 3 days.

INSTRUCTIONS

1. In a medium bowl mix the cornflour and salt.
2. Add one cup of warm water and mix until it's absorbed into the cornflour.
3. Continue adding water until you have a smooth ball of dough. You will know it's ready when it no longer sticks to your hands and it has a smooth consistency.
4. Cover the masa in plastic for 20-30 minutes.
5. Preheat your skillet over medium heat
6. Shape one inch round and place it between the two pieces of plastic on the tortilla press,
7. Place it on a preheated pan and cook for 8-10 seconds on the first side, flip and cook for 20-25 seconds, flip one last time; this time, give it gentle press right in the middle of the tortilla, and it should puff right up right away, Remove it and place it in a tortilla warmer to keep them from getting cold.

PREPARATION: 10MIN
COOKING: 10MIN
READY IN: 20MIN

SOPITA DE FIDEO

By Salty Cocina

INGREDIENTS

- 7 OZ BAG OF FIDEO
- 2 GUAJILLO PEPPERS
- FOUR ROMA TOMATOES
- 1/4 WHITE ONION
- TWO LARGE GARLIC CLOVES
- 1/3 CUP VEGETABLE OIL
- 1 MEDIUM CARROT

- 1 MEDIUM POTATO OF CHOICE
- 2 CUPS OF CHICKEN BROTH
- 1 TBSP CHICKEN BOUILLON OR SALT AS NEEDED
- 6-8 CUPS OF WATER

PREP TIME: 30 MINUTES
COOK TIME: 30 MINUTES
TOTAL TIME: 1 HRS
5-6 SERVINGS

INSTRUCTIONS

1. Peel the garlic, roughly chop the onion and the tomatoes. Peel and dice the carrot and the potato.
2. In a medium saucepan, fry the tomato, onion, garlic, and the guajillo for 2-3 minutes with frequent movement.
3. Remove the pan from the burner, add 2 cups of chicken broth and soak for 5-10 minutes.
4. Blend the ingredients along with the chicken broth.
5. In a separate pot, lightly fry the fideo for 1-2 minutes, add the minced carrot and potato and saute for an additional 1-2 minutes,
6. Add the ingredients from the blender and the chicken bouillon and bring to a simmer. Cover and cook over medium heat for 10-12 minutes
7. Cover for 5-10 minutes before serving

CROCK POT PINTO BEANS

By Salty Cocina

INGREDIENTS

- 2 CUPS PINTO BEANS
- 1 TBSP SALT
- 2 QUARTS WATER
- 3 GARLIC CLOVES
- 1/2 WHIT ONION

PREP TIME: 10 MINUTES
COOK TIME: 6-8 HOURS

INSTRUCTIONS

1. Heat 2 quarts of water in the crockpot.
2. Pick the beans over, removing any damaged, small pieces of debris or misshapen beans and discarding them. Rinse the beans by placing them in a colander and rinsing them thoroughly.
3. Transfer the rinsed beans to a 6-quart or larger slow cooker.
4. Add the onion, garlic, salt, cover, and cook on high for 6-8 hours or until the beans are tender.
5. Once they completely cool down, refrigerate them in an airtight container and use them as needed. Beans can last up to a week in the refrigerator. You can also freeze cooked beans for up to 3 months.

REFRIED BEANS

1. Melt 2-3 tbsp of lard or bacon grease; Saute 1/4 onion, garlic cloves, and two Jalapeños. Add 2-3 cups of beans, 1 cup of broth, and 1 tbsp of chili powder. Mix with an immersion blender, spoon, or potato masher until it reaches your preferred consistency.
2. Simmer over low heat for 8-10 minutes or until it has the thickness you prefer.

FRIED QUESADILLAS

By Salty Cocina

INGREDIENTS

- 2 CUPS CORN FLOUR (MASECA)
- 1 CUP ALL-PURPOSE FLOUR
- 1 TSP SALT
- 1-3/4 - 2 CUPS WARM WATER
- 1/2 LB MOZZARELLA, PEPPER JACK, MONTEREY JACK, MUENSTER, OR YOUR FAVORITE MELTING CHEESE.   VEGETABLE OIL FOR FRYING

Topping Suggestions:
Lettuce, Tomatoes, Queso Cotija,
Sour Cream, Avocado, Salsa

PREPARATION: 10MIN
COOKING: 10MIN
READY IN: 20MIN

INSTRUCTIONS

1. In a medium bowl, mix the cornflour, all-purpose flour, and salt.
2. Add one cup of warm water, mix and continue adding water a little at a time to form a smooth ball of dough; cover with a clean kitchen towel for 10-15 minutes.
3. Form a one-inch ball of dough. Place it between two pieces of plastic, using a flat bottom object or a tortilla press, shape a 4-5 inch round.
4. Remove the top plastic and add grated cheese to one side of the uncooked tortilla. Fold it over, and while the plastic is still on, press down on the sides to seal them. Remove the plastic and make a few more.
5. Heat the vegetable oil and fry each one until golden on both sides,
6. Enjoy with your favorite toppings

CHEESY POTATO TACOS

By Salty Cocina

INGREDIENTS

- 4 RUSSET POTATOES OR A POTATO OF YOUR CHOICE
- 4-5 CHILE GUAJILLO
- 4-5 CHILE DE ARBOL (OPTIONAL)
- 1/2 TSP CUMIN
- 1 TBSP CHICKEN BOUILLON
- 1/4 ONION
- 2 GARLIC CLOVES
- SALT TO YOUR LIKING
- 1 CUP GRATED QUESO OAXACA
- 15 CORN TORTILLAS

PREPARATION: 30
COOKING: 15 MIN
READY IN: 45 MIN

Topping suggestions: lettuce, tomato, avocado, cilantro, queso cotija , and your favorite salsa

INSTRUCTIONS

1. Wash, peel, and dice four potatoes into small bite-size pieces. Boil with a tsp of salt for 10-12 minutes
2. Remove the stems and seed from the chile guajillo and boil with the chile de Arbol for 1-2 minutes. Leave them soaking in hot water until pliable. Blend the peppers with the onion, garlic, cumin, chicken bouillon, and one cup of water.
3. Drain out the water from the potatoes and add the sauce from the blender
4. Using a potato masher, mash the ingredients until it has a smooth, semi-chunky consistency. Taste and add salt or chicken bouillon if needed and mix in the grated cheese.
5. Preheat your corn tortillas in the microwave for a few seconds or until pliable.
6. Add a spoonful of the potatoes to the end of the tortilla and roll it up tightly. Make a few more or as needed.
7. Carefully place each one in the preheated oil with the flap down. Fry on low/med heat until golden on all sides.
8. Enjoy right away with your favorite toppings.

EASY RED RICE

By Salty Cocina

INGREDIENTS

- 2 CUPS LONG GRAIN WHITE RICE
- 4 CUPS WATER
- 8OZ CAN TOMATO SAUCE
- 1/4 MINCED WHITE ONION
- 2 MINCED GARLIC CLOVES
- 3-4 JALAPENOS(OPTIONAL)
- 2 TBSP TOMATO OR CHICKEN BOUILLON
- 1/2 TSP CUMIN
- 1/3 CUP VEGETABLE, CORN, OR CANOLA OIL

PREPARATION: 15 MIN
COOKING: 15 MIN
READY IN: 30 MIN

INSTRUCTIONS

1. Add 2 cups of white rice to a colander and run it under cold water until the water runs clear. Place the colander over a bowl for 10 minutes or until the rice feels dry.
2. Mince the onion and the garlic
3. In a nonstick pan, heat your vegetable oil, add in the rice and lightly toast the rice for about 5-7 minutes over medium heat or lightly toasted.
4. Add in the onion, whole jalapeños, and the garlic and saute for an additional minute.
5. Add in the tomato sauce and saute for about 15-20 seconds before adding the water.
6. Add the chicken bouillon and cumin.
7. Once it reaches a simmer, turn down to low heat and cook with the lid on for about 12 minutes.
8. Keep it covered for ten more minutes before removing the lid.
9. Enjoy your favorite dishes.

CREAMY HATCH CHILE PASTA

By Salty Cocina

INGREDIENTS

- 16 OZ BOX FETTUCCINI OR PREFFERED PASTA
- FIVE HATCH CHILE PEPPERS
- 8 OZ CREAM CHEESE
- 1 CUP HEAVY CREAM
- 2 TSP CHICKEN BOUILLON
- 1/4 ONION
- THREE GARLIC CLOVES
- 1-2 CUP CHICKEN BROTH OR WATER
- 2 TBSP BUTTER

PREP TIME: 30 MINS
COOK TIME: 15 MINS
TOTAL TIME: 45 MINS

INSTRUCTIONS

1. Roast the Hatch Chiles over an open flame, a skillet, pan, in the oven, or an air fryer until blistered and charred. Cool down for 15-20 minutes, then remove the stems, skin, seeds, and veins.
2. Blend the Hatch chiles with cream cheese, onion, garlic, heavy cream, chicken bouillon, and one cup of water or chicken broth.
3. Boil the pasta in 6-8 cups of water with 1 Tsp Salt for 8-10 minutes.
4. In a medium saucepan, melt the butter and add the sauce from the blender.
5. Simmer for 5 minutes, then add in the pasta. Simmer for an additional 3-4 minutes with the pasta. Add chicken broth to adjust the thickness, if needed.

PASTA IN CREAMY CILANTRO SAUCE

By Salty Cocina

INGREDIENTS

- 1/4 WHITE ONION
- 1 GARLIC CLOVE
- 1 SMALL BUNDLE OF CILANTRO
- 1 CUP MEXICAN SOUR CREAM
- 1 CUP JOCOQUE OR BUTTERMILK
- 1-2 TBSP CHICKEN BOUILLON
- 2 CUPS OF CHICKEN BROTH
- 1-1/2 CUP QUESO COTIJA
- 16 OZ BOX OF PENNE PASTA OR YOUR PREFERRED PASTA

INSTRUCTIONS

1. Boil the pasta as instructed on the box
2. Drain the pasta and run it under cold water to stop the cooking process.
3. Blend the garlic, cilantro, sour cream, buttermilk, 1 Tbsp Chicken bouillon, and serrano peppers.
4. In a medium pan, heat one tbsp olive oil, add the sauce and simmer for 5-7 minutes before adding the pasta
5. Simmer for an additional minute with the pasta
6. Remove it from the burner, mix in half a cup of queso cotija and top it off with more cotija cheese; cover for five minutes before serving.
7. Sprinkle with queso cotija before serving.

**MAKES
6-8 SERVINGS**

TINGA TOSTADAS

By Salty Cocina

INGREDIENTS

- 4-5 CUPS OF SHREDDED CHICKEN
- ONE MEDIUM WHITE ONION
- 5 GUAJILLO PEPPERS
- 4-5 CHILES DE ARBOL (OPTIONAL)
- 3 DRY CHIPOTLE PEPPERS OR 1/4 CUP OF CANNED CHIPOTLE PEPPERS
- 4 GARLIC CLOVES
- 3 ROMA TOMATOES
- 1/4 TSP PEPPER
- 1/4 TSP OREGANO
- 2 TBSP CHICKEN BOUILLON OR SALT TO YOUR TASTE
- COOKING OIL (OLIVE OIL, AVOCADO OIL, ETC)

MAKES
8-10 SERVINGS

INSTRUCTIONS

1. Use shredded leftover chicken, rotisserie chicken, or boil 5-6 chicken thighs.
2. Trim off the stems and remove the seeds from the pepper, lightly fry them in a small amount of oil along with half of the onion, roughly chopped tomatoes, and the garlic for 1-2 minutes then add 1 cup of water, cover, and soak for 10-15 minutes.
3. Roughly chop the rest of the onion and saute in 1-2 tbsp of cooking oil for 1-2 minutes then mix in the shredded chicken.
4. Blend the peppers and the rest of the ingredients from the saucepan and add them to the chicken.
5. Add in the seasonings and simmer over low/med heat for 8-10 minutes.
6. Serve on a tostada over a bed of refried beans (optional) and top of with your favorite toppings.

VEGETARIAN TOSTADAS

By Salty Cocina

INGREDIENTS

- 4 YUKON GOLD POTATOES (ANY OTHER TYPE WORKS)
- 4 CHILE GUAJILLO
- 4-5 CHILES DE ARBOL (OPTIONAL)
- 1/4 WHITE ONION
- 1 ROMA TOMATO

- 2 GARLIC CLOVES
- 1/2 TSP CUMIN
- 1/4 TSP BLACK PEPPER
- 1/2 TSP SALT
- 1 TBSP CHICKEN BOUILLON
- 2-3 TBSP VEGETABLE OIL

PREPARATION: 10MIN
COOKING: 20 MIN
READY IN: 30 MIN

INSTRUCTIONS

1. Rinse the tomatoes, the peppers, and remove the seed from the guajillo peppers. Roughly chop the onion and the tomatoes and peel the garlic. Lightly toast them over medium heat for about one minute. Add one cup of water and cover for 10 minutes, then blend along with the water.
2. Wash peel, and dice the potatoes into small bite-sized pieces.
3. Heat the vegetable oil and add the potatoes, season with salt and pepper, and saute for about 2-3 minutes with frequent movement.
4. Add the sauce from the blender, season with cumin and chicken bouillon.
5. Simmer for 5-7 minutes or until the potatoes are tender.
6. Serve on tostadas with your favorite toppings.

LOADED BEEF NACHOS

By Salty Cocina

INGREDIENTS

- 3 GARLIC CLOVES
- 1/2 MEDIUM ONION
- 2-3 JALAPEÑOS OR SERRANO PEPPERS
- 3-4 CUPS OF REFRIED BEANS
- 10 OZ OF CHORIZO OR LONGANIZA
- 14 OZ CAN BEEF BROTH
- TOTOPOS OR TORTILLA CHIPS
- CHEESE (MOZZARELLA, PEPPERJACK, OAXACA (ETC)

- 2-3 LBS FINELY MINCED ROUND STEAK
- 1 LIME
- SALT & PEPPER
- 2-3 TBSP OLIVE OR VEGETABLE OIL
- 2 TBSP CHILI POWDER
- 1 TSP CUMIN
- 1 TSP PAPRIKA

PICO DE GALLO

- 2 SMALL ROMA TOMATOES
- 1-2 SERRANO PEPPERS
- 1/4 RED OR WHITE ONION
- 1/4 BUNDLE OF CILANTRO
- 1 AVOCADO (OPTIONAL)
- SALT AND PEPPER

**PREP TIME:
30 MINUTES
COOK TIME: 30 MINUTES
TOTAL TIME: 1 HR
5-6 SERVINGS**

INSTRUCTIONS

1. Cut the meat into 1-2 inch pieces and transfer to a medium bowl. Pour the oil over the meat and generously season with salt and pepper, squeeze in the juice from one lime, cover, and marinate for 15 minutes.
2. Finely mince the garlic, onion, and jalapeños.
3. In a large skillet, cook the meat over medium-high heat for 10-12 minutes or until it has a light sear.
4. Add in the minced vegetables, chili powder, cumin, and paprika. Cook for an additional 8-10 minutes with frequent movement.
5. In a separate skillet, cook the chorizo for 8-10 minutes, add in the refried beans and one can of beef broth. To add more flavor to the beans, season with garlic and onion powder and salt if needed. Simmer over low heat for 10-12 minutes or until it reaches your desired consistency.

Prepare your nachos by adding a layer of refried beans over the tortilla chips, meat, and cheese. Top them off with pico de gallo, queso cotija, crema Mexicana, or regular sour cream! Before adding the toppings, microwave for a few seconds to melt the cheese.

EASY MOLE RECIPE

By Salty Cocina

INGREDIENTS

- ONE 8.25 OZ BOTTLE OF MOLE DONA MARIA OR YOUR FAVORITE BRAND
- 2-3 LBS OF CHICKEN THIGHS, BREAST, OR LEGS
- 1 ONION (DIVIDED)
- SIX GARLIC CLOVES
- 1/2 TSP CINNAMON
- 1/2 TABLET MEXICAN CHOCOLATE 1/4 CUP CREAMY PEANUT BUTTER
- 1-2 TBSP CHICKEN BOUILLON
- 4-5 CUPS OF CHICKEN BROTH
- 1/2 TBSP SALT
- SESAME SEEDS (OPTIONAL)

INSTRUCTIONS

1. Boil the chicken for 20-25 minutes in 6-8 cups of water, 1/2 onion, three garlic cloves, and 1/2 tbsp of salt.
2. Blend the jar of mole with the remainder of the onion, garlic, chocolate, peanut butter, and 2 cups of chicken broth from the pot.
3. Transfer the ingredients from the blender to a stockpot, add two additional chicken broth cups and bring to s simmer. Simmer over low/med heat for 15-20 minutes or until it reaches your desired consistency. At this point, taste it and add chicken bouillon as needed. Stir frequently to avoid lumps in your sauce.
4. Pour the sauce over the chicken and garnish with sesame seeds.
5. Serve with your favorite red rice, and enjoy!

PREPARATION: 10MIN
COOKING: 30 MIN
READY IN: 40 MIN

CORN TAMALES

By Salty Cocina

INGREDIENTS

- 20 CORN HUSKS
- 8-10 EARS OF CORN OR 6-8 CANS OF CORN
- 2 CUPS CORN FLOUR
- 1 TBSP BAKING POWDER
- 1 TSP BAKING SODA
- 1 TBSP SALT
- 3/4 CUP CORN OIL OR BUTTER
- 1 LB OF YOUR FAVORITE MELTING CHEESE (PEPPER JACK, MONTEREY JACK, MOZZARELLA, CHIHUAHUA CHEESE, ETC.)

SALSA INGREDIENTS

- 6 JALAPEÑOS OR SERRANOS
- 3 ROMA TOMATOES
- 1/4 ONION
- 3 GARLIC CLOVES
- 1 TSP SALT

PREPARATION: 40
COOKING: 1-1/2 HRS
READY IN: 2 1/2 HRS

INSTRUCTIONS

1. Soak 20 corn husks in hot water for 20-30 minutes
2. Over medium-high heat, roast the tomatoes, onion, peppers, and garlic.
3. Using a molcajete or a blender, blend the ingredients and add salt to taste.
4. Dice your cheese into 2-3 inch rectangular shapes.
5. Remove the husk from the corn, place the cob standing up, and slice off downward with a sharp knife to remove the kernels.
6. Grind the kernels in a food processor or blender until lightly coarse and transfer to a bowl.
7. Mix in the cornflour, baking powder, baking soda, oil, and salt.
8. Remove the husks from the pot and drain excess water.
9. Add 3 tbsp of masa in the middle of the husk, a spoonful of salsa, and a stick of cheese. Fold the tamale and continue to prepare the rest.
10. Cook in a steamer on low heat for 1-1 1/2 hours
11. Allow the tamales to cool down for 10 minutes before removing the husk.

BUTTERY JALAPEÑO BREAD

INGREDIENTS

- 2 CUPS ALL-PURPOSE FLOUR
- 2 1/4 TSP FAST ACTING DRY YEAST (1 PACKET)
- 1 TBSP SUGAR
- 1 TSP SALT
- 2 LARGE EGG

- 1/2 CUP WARM MILK
- 3 TBSP MELTED BUTTER
- 3/4 CUP MEXICAN BLEND CHEESE OR CHEDDAR JACK
- 1/2 CUP DICED PICKLED JALAPENOS

PREP TIME: TIME: 2 1/2 HRS
COOK TIME: 30 MINUTES
TOTAL TIME: 3 HRS
18-10 SERVINGS

INSTRUCTIONS

1. Activate the yeast in warm milk, one tbsp of sugar, two tbsp of flour, and mix until it's lump-free. Cover and place in a warm, dry place for 8-10 minutes or until it doubles in volume.
2. Mix in the activated yeast with the flour along with the butter, one egg, and salt.
3. Using a spatula, mix until all the ingredients, the dough should feel a little sticky.
4. Cover the bowl with plastic for 1 hour or until it doubles in volume.
5. Transfer the dough to a lightly floured working surface and gently fold it to create a smooth ball of dough. Flatten it out by hand to a 4-5 inch round, and using a rolling pin, roll it out until you have a 12-15 inch round.
6. Spread 2-3 Tbsp of room temperature butter over the dough
7. Evenly spread the pickled jalapeños over the butter and 1/2 a cup of the cheese.
8. Spray an 8'x4' round baking pan with butter or cooking spray.
9. Using a pizza cutter, slice the dough into triangular shapes (it's okay if they are different sizes)
10. Roll each piece into a small croissant and arrange them in the baking pan by placing the larger pieces on the bottom and using the smaller pieces to fill in the gaps.
11. Cover with a plastic or clean kitchen towel and place it in a warm, dry place for 30 minutes or until it doubles in volume.
12. Scramble the second egg and brush the egg over the bread, making sure to get all the nooks and crannies and sprinkle with the remainder of the cheese.
13. Bake at 350 degrees for 30 minutes
14. Cool down for 10-15 minutes before removing it from the pan

HOMEMADE BOLILLOS

By Salty Cocina

INGREDIENTS

- 3 CUPS ALL-PURPOSE FLOUR (EXTRA FLOUR FOR DUSTING)
- 1 PACKET ACTIVE DRY YEAST (2 1/4 TSP)
- 1 1/4 CUPS WARM MILK
- 2 TBSP SUGAR
- 1 TSP SALT
- 4 TBSP BUTTER (OR 1/4 CUP MELTED SHORTENING OR LARD
- VEGETABLE SHORTENING FOR THE BOWL

PREP TIME: TIME: 3 HRS
COOK TIME: 20 MINUTES
TOTAL TIME: 3 1/2 TO 4 HRS
MAKES 8-10 MEDIUM SIZE BOLILLOS

INSTRUCTIONS

1. Activate the yeast in 1-1/4 cups of warm milk, one tbsp sugar, and two tbsp flour. Cover and place in a warm, dry place for 10-15 minutes or until it doubles in volume.
2. Mix the sugar and salt with the flour.
3. Mix in the melted butter and the activated yeast
4. If using a stand-up mixer, mix on medium-high speed for 8-10 minutes; you will know it's ready when the dough has come together, and it no longer sticks to the side of your bowl; the dough should have some elasticity.
5. Transfer the dough to a clean working surface and shape it into a smooth ball of dough.
6. Grease a large bowl with shortening or oil. Place the dough in the bowl and turn it over to ensure all sides are oiled. Cover with plastic wrap and rest in a warm place for 1-2 hours or until it doubles in volume.
7. Using your fist, press down on the dough to remove the air and divide the dough into equal-sized pieces.
8. Roll each ball on a lightly floured working surface, tapering the ends to create an oblong shape.
9. Place the bolillos in an ungreased cookie sheet, cover with plastic wrap, or a clean kitchen towel for 30-45 minutes.
10. Preheat your oven to 425 degrees
11. Once the rolls have doubled in volume, make a slit on top of each bolillo using a sharp knife.
12. Spray the bolillos with warm water and place them in the preheated oven. Fill a separate baking dish with 2-3 cups of hot water and put it right underneath the bolillos. The steam from the warm water is going to give them a light, crunchy crust.
13. Bake for 12-15 minutes or until golden

ARROZ CON LECHE

By Salty Cocina

INGREDIENTS

- 3/4 CUP OF WHITE RICE
- 2 CUPS OF WATER
- 1 STICK OF CINNAMON
- ORANGE PEEL FROM ONE ORANGE
- 14 OZ CAN CONDENSED MILK
- 12 OZ CAN EVAPORATED MILK
- 4 CUPS OF WHOLE MILK
- GROUND CINNAMON FOR GARNISHING

PREP TIME: TIME: 10 MINUTES

COOK TIME: 30 MINUTES

TOTAL TIME: 40 MINUTES

5-6 SERVINGS

INSTRUCTIONS

1. Rinse the rice until the water runs clear.
2. In a medium saucepan, bring two cups of water to a simmer, add the rice and the cinnamon stick, and boil for 5-7 minutes over medium heat.
3. Before most of the water simmers down, add the peel of one orange with the least amount of white rind (I used the entire peel and removed it out before serving)
4. Add whole milk, condensed milk, and evaporated milk and simmer over low, medium heat for 12-15 minutes, frequently stirring, so it doesn't stick to the bottom of the saucepan.
5. Cover for at least 10-15 minutes before serving

MOSAIC TRES LECHES JELLO

By Salty Cocina

INSTRUCTIONS

1. Prepare the jello as instructed for jello jigglers. Refrigerate in a square-shaped dish for 3 hours or until set.
2. Cut the gelatin into 1/2 inch pieces.
3. Dissolve the four envelopes of unflavored gelatin in one cup of warm water.
4. In a large bowl, combine the evaporated milk, condensed milk, cream, one teaspoon of vanilla, then mix in the unflavored gelatin.
5. Lightly grease the bundt pan with cooking spray or vegetable oil.
6. Arrange the jello in the bundt cake and pour in the milk mixture over the jello.
7. Cover and refrigerate for 6-8 hours or until set.
8. Before removing it from the bundt pan, press down on the side of the jello to release it from the mold.
9. Place a plate over the bund cake and very carefully flip it over.
10. Serve with whip cream or by itself.

INGREDIENTS

- Two 6oz Jello (Any Flavor)
- 6 Cups Hot Water (Divided)
- 12 oz Can Evaporated Milk
- 14 Oz Can Condensed Milk
- 1 Tsp Vanilla
- 7.6 oz Can Mexican Cream or 1 Cup Heavy Cream
- 1 oz Box Unflavored Gelatin(each box contains four envelopes) Use all four

Other Ingredients Needed:
Cooking Spray or Vegetable Shortening for the Bundt Pan

PREPARATION: 10MIN
COOKING: 10MIN
READY IN: 20MIN

MOST COMMON SPICES USED IN MEXICAN COOKING

Mexico has an abundance of spices and herbs that traditional cooks have used for centuries.
So if you're looking to create better-tasting, traditional Mexican food, we put together a list of the most frequently used Mexican spices, herbs, and chiles to take your meal to the next level.

Chile Guajillo is one of the most popular peppers used in Mexican cuisine. They offer a sweet, lightly smoky flavor with very little to no heat. Great for preparing sauces, mole marinades, soups, stews, and much more. When shopping for guajillo peppers, choose those with smooth, shiny skin—pliable Peppers indicating freshness.

How to use: soak in hot water until pliable or lightly toast it over medium heat to add richness and a light smokey flavor.

Ancho/Pasilla Peppers is the dry form of poblano peppers. Its smoky quality with a hint of paprika flavor and its sweet to mild heat; these peppers add color and flavor to sauces and pastes.

How to use: Ancho peppers require rehydrating before using. The process involves removing the stem and the seeds then soaking them in boiling water for 20-30 minutes or until pliable.

Ancho peppers are made by allowing the Poblano Peppers to ripen on the vine until they turn a bright red; they are harvested and dried to preserve the pepper.

Mulato Pepper is dried poblanos similar to ancho peppers but with a slightly different flavor. While both are green while growing, Mulatos are left on the vine to ripen to a brown color. This pepper carries very little heat, and the best way to describe the taste of this pepper is a combination of chocolate, licorice, and cherry.

How to use: Prepare mole sauce, along with the ancho, pasilla, and guajillo peppers.

Chile Puya is a smaller, spicier version of the guajillo. They measure 4-5 inches in length and look very similar to chiles de Arbol, except larger. They're thin, bright red, and a little rugged.

How to use: Once they're toasted, you can cool them and grind them into a chili powder for sprinkling onto foods to add a dose of heat, add them to stews and sauces like you would with guajillos.

Chile de Arbol is very popular in Mexican and Asian cuisine, also known as "bird beak chiles" or "rat's tail chiles," it's a tiny thin pepper with a smoky acid flavor. It also packs much heat, which is about six times hotter than the jalapeño pepper. Use these firery peppers in homemade salsas, chili, or any other dish you want to add extra heat.

How to use: soak in hot water until pliable or lightly toast them to bring out the heat.

Dry Chipotle Peppers are left on the vine until they ripen to a red, then they are harvested and smoked until dry. They hold a good level of heat, similar to a jalapeño. The dry version of chipotle peppers adds a spicy smokiness to any dish.

How to use: rehydrate them to make chili paste or grind them to make chipotle chili powder for salsas, chilis, or other dishes.

Dry Chile Tepin is an intensely hot pepper ranking high in heat, nicknamed "bird's eye" peppers. Some say that the Tepin is more desirable than the habanero pepper. This pepper is round or slightly oval and about 3/8 inch in width.

How to use: Grind them into *the coarse texture flakes or powder. Rehydrate them by soaking them in hot water for about 15 minutes. Use them in dishes or salsas to add extra heat.*
-For best results, dry toast them to enhance the flavor and spice —store chile tepin in an airtight container for up to a year.

Habanero Pepper is a fiery chili pepper with a fruity, citrusy flavor. They are small, typically 1–2 inches wide. Depending on the variety, they start the green on the plant but mature to a vibrant orange or red.

How to use: This pepper is famous for its heat, making it the perfect pepper to use when making salsas or any other dish you want o add heat.

Poblano Peppers are typically 4 inches long and are very dark green in color. Poblanos peppers are very mild in flavor, making them popular in Mexican cuisine. **How to Use:** They are roasted, peeled, and used for various dishes, including chile rellenos, chiles en nogada, rajas con queso, and many other recipes.

Serrano Peppers *get their name from the* mountain ridge of Mexico, where they originated. This small pointy pepper adds a sharp and fiery heat flavor to Mexican and Asian cuisine. **How to use:** Can be eaten raw, cooked, or pickled or add it to dishes to add extra heat. The heat is in the seeds and inner flesh, so the seeds and inner flesh are occasionally scraped out for less heat.

Jalapenos America's favorite chili peppers were initially grown in Xalapa, the capital of Vera Cruz, Mexico. These peppers range from mild to very hot; small ridges can sometimes mean it is spicy. More significant than average jalapeños tend to be very low on the spice level. **How to use:** Add seeded jalapenos to soups, stews, dips, whole, or roasted to prepare jalapeño poppers.

Fun Fact: *Did you know jalapeños pack more vitamin C than an orange? They also contain Carotene, which is an antioxidant that may help fight damage to your cells. They also have Capsaicin, which is thermogenic that stimulates the body's burning of fat.*

Mexican Oregano is an all-purpose seasoning found in just about any Latin American kitchen. Mexican oregano is entirely different from what we consider "regular" oregano, Mediterranean oregano is sweet, with anise notes, and Mexican oregano is grassy, with citrus notes. Commonly used in pozole, menudo, salsas, tacos, and stews,

Anise is not star-anise, though the names are somewhat similar. They belong to different plant families. Anise and fennel are from the same family and are closely related to flavor. Used in sweet and savory dishes, including baked goods like sugar cookies, sweetbread, and biscuits. Anise also tastes like black licorice.

Star Anise - is a star-shaped seed pod from an evergreen tree, which is native to China. While technically not related to regular anise, this spice does have a similar flavor. Anise has a robust and medicinal licorice flavor, while star anise is sweeter - more identical to fennel than licorice. You can also use the entire pods for spiced apple cider, Mexican Christmas punch, desserts, and Mexican chocolate or champurrado.

Piloncillo is the most common name for this type of sugar in Mexico, but it is also known as panocha or panela in other Latin and Central American countries. Piloncillo is unrefined Mexican sugar made from cane sugar made from boiling and evaporating cane juice. Use it to replace white or brown sugar in baking and desserts. , Some of the most popular Mexican recipes are champurrado, capirotada, cafe de olla, and even savory dishes!

Achiote Paste is a combination of crushed achiote seed, vinegar, salt, garlic, and spices typically formed into a small block. The paste is then diluted and added to stews or rubs for meats and marinades, including cochinita pibil, tacos al pastor, seafood, and chicken.

Annato - The orange-red seeds of the annatto tree, native to the tropical areas of the Americas. Dry seeds are grounded to a powder or made into a paste. It is a primary spice in Yucatan, Mexico, used in savory dishes and stews. Its flavor is sweet and earthy, and it pairs well with citrus.

Coriander seeds - come from the cilantro plant. These tiny spheres have a sweet, earthy, and citrusy aroma heightened by toasting gently before use and often used in pickling, legumes, stews.

Cumin - is a classic spice in Mexican cuisine that can be found whole or grounded. Cumin tastes slightly bitter and has a robust toasty flavor. It can modify any dish, even in small quantities. Used in rice dishes, stews, soups, sauces, and chili con carne recipes.

Thyme- has a dry, fresh, pungent flavor that complements the heat in many Mexican dishes—commonly used in soups, sauces, salads, and dressings.

Allspice or Pimienta Gorda-
It is native to Latin America and the Caribbean. The taste combines a fragrant aroma and the flavors of cinnamon, ginger, cloves, and nutmeg. It also pairs nicely to compliment all of those spices. Often used as a pickling spice in adobos and pipian sauce, but is also common in desserts, cookies, casseroles, and meat recipes.

Cinnamon/Mexican Canela -
tastes pungent and woodsy because it is the inner bark of a tree. Mexican cinnamon, Canela, was first introduced by the Spanish conquistadores. Widely used in Mexican cuisine and is commonly used to prepare moles, meat recipes, marinades, desserts, horchata, rice pudding, dulce de leche, and Mexican hot chocolate. It pairs well with vegetables like carrots and winter squashes.

Nutmeg -
It gives a warm taste similar to cinnamon and cloves; nutmeg can be used whole or grounded and commonly used in Mole Poblano, baked goods, medicinal purposes, and Mexican hot chocolate.

Chili Powder -
is a blend of mild chili peppers, such as ancho, guajillo, or New Mexico peppers. Its bold taste makes it popular in Mexican and Southwestern dishes such as stews, chilis, chilaquiles, and everyday cooking. Its bold taste adds a light heat that is not overwhelming.

Cloves - also known as "clavos de olor," translates to "nails that smell," the distinct peppery-sweet flavor, pairs well with cumin or cinnamon. You can find this spice in cafe de olla, savory dishes, drinks, mole, and desserts. Use them grounded or whole but always in a small amount. Clove is known to be a good anesthetic, and in many households in Mexico, they will use it as a pain reliever for toothaches.

Garlic - is among the most common flavors you will find in Mexican food. It comes fresh, in a jar, or powdered form. Use it in many recipes like salsa, taco seasoning, rice, meats, soups, and stews are just a few recipes that rely heavily on garlic.

Bay Leaf - are used fresh or dried in cooking for their distinctive flavor and fragrance. Its flavor is slightly floral, herbal, and a bit bitter, similar to oregano and marjoram. In Mexico, it is used extensively in soups, stews, broths, and rice.

Pepper - the world's most important spice, peppercorns are the small, round berries of a climbing vine native to southwestern India. Use whole peppercorns in making stock and ground pepper to season the outside of the meat, poultry, and fish. For better results, invest in a decent pepper grinder and throw away the pre-ground stuff. Whole peppercorns are an essential ingredient in Mexican pickled chiles.

Epazote - While technically a herb, epazote in its dry form is used as a spice. The plant is native to Mexico and Central and South America. Its flavor is pungent with notes of anise, oregano, citrus, and mint. It is used primarily to flavor black beans or in sauces. It is said that cooking beans with epazote aids in digestion (aka reducing the gas they often cause).

Mexican Vanilla - offers rich, sweet, and woody notes with deep, spicy characters. Its clove and nutmeg-like qualities provide a flavorful culinary twist to all of your favorite recipes, such as baked goods, agua frescas, desserts, and smoothies!

Hibiscus - or flor de Jamaica, is deep red in color. It has sweet and tart flavors, similar to cranberry. The dry flowers are great in tea or use them to make marinades for meats, taco filling, jellies, and it also pairs well with chiles and cheese for a twist on a vegetarian quesadilla.

They are not just delicious, but they also contain antioxidants, Vitamin C, excellent for your liver and digestive system, and it's a natural diuretic and helps reduce bloating.

When you think of Mexican food, chances are, there's cheese involved. The salty, tangy, creamy, and rich flavors offset the dishes' heat, spice and add much flavor to any dish,
We have put a list together of the most popular Mexican Cheeses and when and how to use them. You will also find a recipe for a homemade queso fresco!

QUESO DE OAXACA

Oaxaca is one of the most popular cheeses in Mexico and originates from Oaxaca, Mexico. This semi-soft cheese has a similar texture to mozzarella cheese and has a mellow, salty flavor. The ball knot form is made by stretching the cheese curds into long strings, and then the strings are wound into a ball. It melts well and is used for stuffing peppers, quesadillas, nachos, queso fundido, and enchiladas. Substitutions can include Monterey Jack, provolone, and mozzarella.

QUESO FRESCO

Queso fresco translates to fresh cheese made from raw cow's milk or a combination of goat and cow milk. This cheese has a very mild flavor and tastes similar to feta cheese. Crumble over beans, enchiladas, chiles rellenos, or any other dish you want to add flavor to!

HOMEMADE QUESO FRESCO

By Salty Cocina

Ingredients

- ONE GALLON WHOLE MILK
- 1/2 CUP WHITE VINEGAR
- 1 TSP SALT

INSTRUCTIONS

1. In a large pot, heat the milk over medium-high heat to 190°F or right before it reaches the boiling point. Turn off the burner and gradually add in the vinegar. Mix slightly and cover for 30 minutes while the separation finishes.
2. Using a larger pot or bowl, place a strainer over the pot or bowl and line the colander with four layers of cheesecloth.
3. Carefully pour the hot mixture into the colander. The liquid whey can be reserved and used for other recipes, or you can discard it. Allow the cheese to drain in the colander for 20-30 minutes to remove the excess whey. (Speed up the process by placing a large, heavy object over the curds)
4. Transfer cheese to a small bowl, add the salt and mix until it's well combined. Cover with plastic wrap and refrigerate for at least 6 hours or overnight.

Queso Cotija Has a strong and salty flavor with a sharp smell and a crumbly texture, often referred to as the Parmesan of Mexico. The word "Cotija" refers to the Cotija municipality in Michoacán, Mexico, from where the cheese originates. It doesn't melt when cooked, so it's best used as a topper cheese: broken down into bits and sprinkled over the top of enchiladas, wet burritos, tostadas, enchiladas, salads, dips, capirotada, elotes, or any dish you want to add a little flavor.

Homemade Queso Cotija

Ingredients

- ONE GALLON OF SKIM MILK
- 1/2 CUP VINEGAR OR LEMON JUICE
- SALT TO TASTE

Instructions

1. In a medium stockpot, heat the skim milk until it reaches 90 degrees Celsius or right before it reaches the boiling point. Make sure to stir frequently during the process.
2. Once it reaches the right temperature, remove it from the burner and add vinegar or lemon juice. Give it a few stirs, cover the stockpot and let it rest for 30-45 minutes.
3. Line a strainer with four layers of cheesecloth, squeeze the cheesecloth to remove any excess whey.
4. Transfer the cheese to a bowl and mix in the salt.
5. Pack the cheese into a cheese mold, cover with plastic and refrigerate for 3-7 days.
6. Queso cotija is aged cheese; the longer it is stored, the better the results.
7. Enjoy with your favorite dishes!

PANELA CHEESE

Panela cheese gets its name for the "canastas de pan" or bread baskets, in which it's how traditionally drained and pressed. Prepared with skim milk, it is firmer and considerably more flexible than queso fresco. It can be easily cut but not crumbled, and It has a slightly rubbery texture. Panela cheese is somewhat salty, and it can be used as a snack or cut up into a salad or sliced thick for sandwiches. Panela cheese does not melt, which makes it perfect for frying.

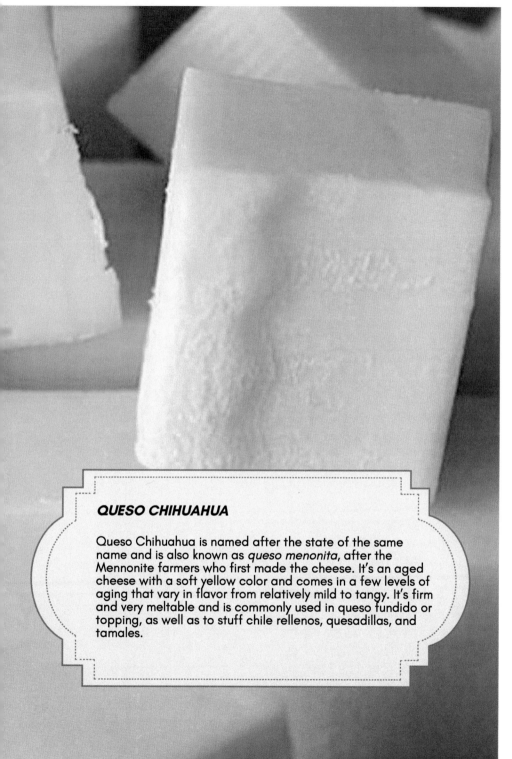

QUESO CHIHUAHUA

Queso Chihuahua is named after the state of the same name and is also known as *queso menonita*, after the Mennonite farmers who first made the cheese. It's an aged cheese with a soft yellow color and comes in a few levels of aging that vary in flavor from relatively mild to tangy. It's firm and very meltable and is commonly used in queso fundido or topping, as well as to stuff chile rellenos, quesadillas, and tamales.

FRIED QUESO PANELA WITH ROASTED TOMATILLO SALSA

By Salty Cocina

INGREDIENTS

- 5 TOMATILLOS, HUSKED, WASHED, AND HALVED
- 3-4 SERRANOS PEPPERS
- HALF A BUNCH OF ROUGHLY CHOPPED CILANTRO
- 1 LIME
- 1 TEASPOON FRESHLY MINCED GARLIC FROM ABOUT 1 MEDIUM CLOVE
- SALT AND PEPPER, TO TASTE
- 1 SMALL YELLOW OR WHITE ONION (DIVIDED)
- 12 OUNCES QUESO PANELA, CUT INTO 1/2-INCH SLICES
- CORN TORTILLAS, FOR SERVING

INSTRUCTIONS

1. Peel the tomatillos, wash them and cut them in half, remove the stems from the serrano peppers, roughly chop the onion, and peel the garlic.
2. Over medium heat, lightly fry the tomatillos and peppers for 5 minutes, then add the garlic and onion and fry for an additional minute.
3. Finely chop the onion and the cilantro and place them in a bowl.
4. Blend the ingredients with 1/4 cup water, add it to the bowl with the onion and cilantro.
5. Slice the Panela cheese into 2-inch slices and fry them over low/med on all sides.
6. Serve over a bed of tomatillo salsa and enjoy with warm corn tortillas.

REQUESÓN

Requesón is soft, creamy, mild, and is a lower-fat cheese, making it ideal for enchilada filling, lasagna, breakfast recipes, and desserts! Often referred to as "Hispanic Ricotta" style cheese. Substitute for Requesón: Ricotta Cheese

99

CREMA MEXICANA

Not a cheese but a dairy staple in Mexican cuisine. So what is the difference between sour cream and Mexican cream? Sour cream has a fat content of about 20% and is relatively thick, and it also tends to curdle when used in hot preparation.
Mexican crema has a higher fat content of about 30%; it's sourer and thinner. It does not curdle, making it perfect for mixing hot dishes. It is incredibly versatile, complements spicy food, salty food, and sweet foods. It's often a finishing touch to Mexican dishes like tacos, enchiladas, and mixed into soups. In addition to adding great flavor, it also helps tone down the heat and spiciness of chiles used in Mexican cuisine.
You can find it in most supermarkets in the dairy section. If you cannot find crema Mexicana in your local store, you can make this simple version at home.

HOMEMADE CREMA MEXICANA

By Salty Cocina

INGREDIENTS

- 1 Cup Sour Cream
- 1/2 Cup Buttermilk
- Salt to Taste
- 1 Tsp Lime Juice

INSTRUCTIONS

1. In a small bowl, mix the sour cream with salt and lime juice.
2. Mix in the buttermilk a little at a time until it reaches your desired thickness.
3. Cover and use as needed.

Made in the USA
Las Vegas, NV
23 January 2022

42128960R00062